Radical Fashion Ex

MW00609748

Laura Gardner & Daphne Mohajer va Pesaran (eds.)

radical fashion exercises

a workbook of modes and methods

Valiz

radical p

exercises

introduct

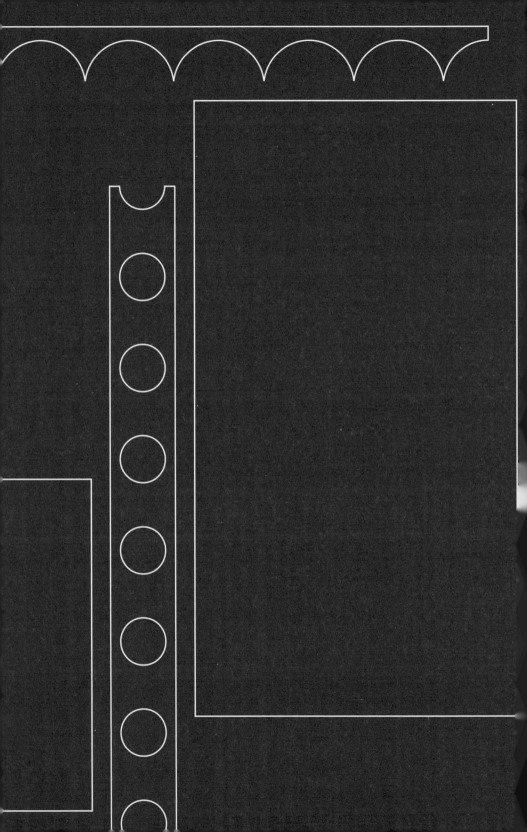

All fashion designers and practitioners need to be radicals.

Radical Fashion Exercises is a workbook that promotes radicality within a fashion system that is coercively commercial. This book invites participation, research, and making to radically rethink fashion in relation to history, community, ecology, social good, and the longer impact of design.

Within its pages, you will find a collection of exercises and invitations to action by fashion and textiles practitioners, makers, educators, curators, artists, and researchers from around the world. Some are speculative and challenging, while others are direct and accessible. Above all, the exercises promote new ways of doing fashion through participation and direct action and aim to destabilize the self-reinforcing power structures of the twenty-first century fashion industry.

The garments we make and wear—from the ubiquitous white T-shirt to cutting-edge runway fashion—have become potent symbols of extraction and exploitation. In its wake, fashion leaves behind contamination, injustice, and waste. Critics say the fashion system is broken; but for some, the system is working exactly as intended. This monolithic system feels immutable: it can seem as though change is not only unlikely but structurally impossible. Despite this, we know that the fashion industry needs radical change.

But what is a 'radical' fashion practice? Radicality is antagonistic, working in opposition to hierarchical and dominant structures. The word 'radical' as we deploy it in this book means 'supporting change'. In other words, believing or expressing the belief that there should be great or extreme social or political change. Radical can be defined as 'very important/extreme', as in: 'we need to make some radical changes to our operating procedures'.[1] It could be said that fashion already operates in dynamics of major upheaval, given the new visual and material changes inherent to every seasonal presentation. We argue that the genuinely radical changes required to shift the trajectory of current fashion start not in aesthetic novelty but with the reform of fashion's 'operating procedures' and in more active, fundamental ways that precede the expression of fashion. In other words, how projects begin, how design practice is learned, how fashion

1   Cambridge English Dictionary, 'Radical.'
     Cambridge English Dictionary (Cambridge:
     Cambridge University Press). www.dictionary.
     cambridge.org/dictionary/english/radical

is experienced. We would like to offer a radical (if paradoxical) provocation here: all fashion designers and practitioners need to be radicals. In its form and in its ethics, industrial fashion requires a sustained and agonistic critique—a critique that operates creatively at the point of production: we want *more* fashion, more equity, more difference, more self-consciousness, and more collectivity.

This belief arises from our work at the Royal Melbourne Institute of Technology (RMIT) University in Melbourne, Australia, where our approach to teaching is diverging from the industry-standard technical approaches we experienced in our own fashion undergraduate degrees some years ago. We are led by our students, who understand they must look at fashion critically and urgently, and are questioning and exploring more inclusive, ethical, and circular modes of practice.

Radical Fashion Exercises is an expression of a critical optimism. The book's contributors engage with fashion not simply as a commercial product, but as an expanded and complex historical, social, and economic concept connected to everyday life. These fashion methods are interdisciplinary, grass-roots, engage critical reflection, research, activism, collective making, re-use, and invite direct action to resist commercial and capitalist fashion. They aim to empower you—the wearer, designer, consumer, student, researcher, and maker—to optimistically imagine an alternative, more equitable, and environmentally responsible vision of fashion.

The collection of exercises in this workbook draws from people who are imagining an alternative future for industrial fashion. These individuals contribute to experimental fashion practice in the radical peripheries of the industry, if even on a small, micro scale. In these peripheries, industrial fashion is not settled or fixed; its meaning is contested, expanded, and troubled. A fashion system more aware of its capacities and consequences is possible and the only way to bring it into being is through radical, collective action.

This project began in late 2021, when we called for critical fashion practitioners to submit an exercise that would 're-imagine fashion as a design process, product, and symbolic form'. We received over 360 submissions; an international panel honed these down to the 102 exercises you find in this book.

We have structured the book into nine themes: 'Imagining and Dreaming', 'Going Outside', 'Using the Body', 'Working Together', 'Reading and Writing', 'Making, Finding, Tracing',

'Re-viewing Images', 'Digging Deep' and 'Sourcing and Re-sourcing'. These themes constitute key sites of change that connect across fashion practices, from amateur, to education, industry, and research. They represent territory where the practice of fashion is undergoing an upheaval of historical traditions. We see this, for instance, in the way garment making and construction is taught.

The theme 'Imagining and Dreaming' asks the reader to envision alternative and speculative worlds of fashion as a premise for design and to think through the dynamics of fashion in the present. The theme 'Going Outside' collects hands-on and experiential approaches to looking at fashion by sending the reader on an excursion to the places and spaces of fashion and its retail culture. 'Using the Body' asks the reader to examine the living, sensing, moving bodies that we inhabit and that give life to our garments as a creative mechanism to generate design outcomes. The theme 'Working Together' focuses on collectivity, participation, and collaboration as a method not only for sharing knowledge, but of making together. The theme of 'Reading and Writing' gathers methods of experimental and poetic writing, critique, and storytelling to evaluate the way that fashion is constructed and sold through language and text. Some of the exercises under this theme turn fashion text on its head altogether by using it as the starting point for garment or form. The theme 'Making, Finding, Tracing' surveys new methods that break from the traditions and rules of the making process and how garments are draped, patterns are made, and garments constructed. 'Re-viewing Images' looks at the fashion image, the lingua franca of fashion, as a site for change. Exercises in this theme question and dissect images, their role as the language of the fashion industry, and the social values they promote. The theme of 'Digging Deep' contains methods of deep research and analysis, excavating fashion histories (and the potential inequities of these histories) towards a more meaningful engagement with the present conditions of fashion. 'Sourcing and Re-sourcing' looks more specifically at methods facilitating a more circular supply chain and sourcing as a creative process. Under this theme, exercises review raw materials and waste and offer methods for reusing, salvaging, and remaking.

The exercises themselves do not follow a set structure and are written in the idiosyncratic voices of their authors. In the same way, they invite interpretation, experimentation, and aesthetic play. We encourage you to make these exercises your own, adapt them to fit your work and its methods. Many of the exercises also ask the reader to work with others. Collaboration within the discipline of fashion and with other disciplines is an essential skill this book aims to promote. We need to build communities of resistance to dominant fashion.

Accordingly, we tried to keep a balance across the themes and different approaches in fashion. The open call method naturally meant that we had an abundance of certain methods above others. We were overwhelmed, for example, by exercises for reuse, material affordances, and circularity, suggesting this to be a particularly pertinent mode of practice and teaching at the moment. We recognize that there are also under-represented areas of contemporary fashion practice in the exercises gathered here—in particular, the territory of gender and sexuality. This does not reflect the significance of the topic in fashion today, but perhaps more the challenge of distilling such a topic into an exercise. We also note that while only a few of the exercises address the realm of digital practices (since the printed format isn't the ideal place to explore this medium), digitality/networked cultures are embedded in many of the exercises. Furthermore, this book does not have a specific section dedicated to sustainability or social ethics: instead, we feel that these values should be fundamental in every practice and project we have included.

Radical Fashion Exercises is a book of exercises and invitations that is, in a sense, incomplete without an active reader. It is a book of methods, ideas, and actions for the reader to set in motion and radicalize fashion. As much as it is a book about 'doing', it is also about 'thinking'. Its exercises and activities, though short, should also invite deep consideration and discussion about alternatives to some of the problems facing fashion, how it is produced, and how we consume it. The book also invites questioning, research, and criticism. It often asks the reader to question fashion's politics and economics, but also to look inward at their own wardrobe or bodies. The exercises can be developed into longer engagements if paired together, or if bookended with time for discussion and reflection.

In this way, *Radical Fashion Exercises* is inspired by the prospect of the book as a mobile, flexible mechanism for collective and autonomous education, whether inside or outside of the industry or institution. We are stimulated by the counter-cultural traditions of DIY and the recent publications that add to this tradition. In particular, books such as *Taking a Line for a Walk: Assignments in Design Education* edited by Nina Paim and Emilia Bergmark[2] and *Wicked Art Assignments: Practising Creativity in Contemporary Arts Education* edited by Emiel Heijnen and Melissa Bremmer,[3] offer concrete methods for teaching and practicing art and design.[4] These books give readers the tools not just for making and doing, but simultaneously thinking through their respective disciplines.

The exercises in this book are not complete methodologies for design. Rather, they are starting points, invitations, and openings to allow you to get somewhere new. On each page you will find a way to do something, a method for investigation that could contribute to your overall way of thinking, or a strategy for how you engage with fashion, whether you are an artist, designer, researcher, or other. Some are simple provocations (as in Annie Wu's invitation to make a wardrobe while on vacation with only materials sourced locally); others are parts of a wider, more sophisticated approach to design that invite you to explore and create your own path (such as Martine Rose's exercise, which invites you to tell stories about people). These methods will allow you to go beyond the mannequins, moodboards, and logos of fashion education. They can partner with how you already work, amplify your feelings and thoughts about how things could be, contribute to the development of a new way to do research or learn about fashion, or lead you into something other than a career in the fashion industry by opening up a completely new model of fashion practice. They will not dictate a specific outcome— you will.

These radical fashion exercises are for the fashion radical: someone willing to change the 'operating procedures' of the fashion industry. We invite you to take up your tools, think radically, and turn the page.

2   Nina Paim and Emilia Bergmark (ed.), *Taking a Line for a Walk: Assignments in Design Education* (Leipzig: Spector Books, 2016).

3   Emiel Heijnen and Melissa Bremmer, *Wicked Art Assignments: Practising Creativity in Contemporary Arts Education* (Amsterdam: Valiz, 2021).

4   It is also worth mentioning the titles: *Draw it with Your Eyes Closed: The Art of the Art Assignment* edited by Dushko Petrovich and Roger White (Brooklyn: Paper Monument, 2012); *A New Program for Graphic Design* by David Reinfurt (Los Angeles Inventory Press, 2019); *Opening up the Wardrobe: A Methods Book* by Kate Fletcher and Ingun Grimstad Klepp (Oslo: Novus Press, 2017); and *Artistic Development in [Fashion] Design* (2010) by Clemens Thornquist (Leiden: Center for Textiles Research, 2010)

and

The fashion industry is a factory of dreams. These dreams can be aspirational and even utopian, but this hopefulness can sometimes obscure the nightmare of the dystopian social and material realities hidden within. Fashion dreams—whether utopian or dystopian—are productive and can speculate on the future of fashion and the poetics of possibility. The exercises in 'Imagining and Dreaming' invite us to consider alternative visions in order to think through the present conditions of fashion. For instance, Amy Twigger Holroyd's 'Fashion Fictions' imagines the fashion system of an alternate present. Julie Gork's 'Body Evolutions' asks us to speculate on a future, post-human body and how it might be clothed.

In his essay 'Lumbar Thought', Umberto Eco writes evocatively that, 'in imposing an exterior demeanour, clothes are semiotic devices, machines for communicating'.[1] In other words, fashion is an embodied phenomenon that conversely influences how we think and imagine ourselves. This theme also contains methods that deal with fashion as a performance of character and social presentation. These exercises creatively explore fashion as a signifier and mode of communication for social and personal values. Valerie Lange's 'Know Your Enemy' asks us to become intimate and up-close with the psyche of an 'enemy', to understand their motivations by wearing their garments. PAGEANT's 'Fashion Relic' is another method for exploring the personas of garments and thus the people that wear them. It asks us to imagine the previous wearer of a second-hand garment to explore the experience of wear and its psychological and physiological effects.

1   Eco, Umberto. 'Lumbar thought.' In *Fashion Theory* (Oxfordshire: Routledge, 2017) 317.

connections

Making a collection is a constant reimagining of the friends, lovers, people on the bus, thinkers, jokers, and characters that affect our lives. Familiarity viewed through the lens of a funhouse mirror—familiar, yet skewed. Whether it's compiling the research for a collection or editing its fabric selection. 'Double or single breasted? Do I want to hang out with this person, sleep with this person, share my life with this person? Do I already know them?'

Our collections are about the everyday and the ordinary and, most of all, about people.

Go and find six people you don't know—who, for whatever reason, engage and inspire you. It could be the way that they wear their hair, how they move, what they wear or what they have to share/say. Photograph them if possible, or describe to yourself the essence of what was special about them. Find a way to reinterpret that mood with bits of fabric, objects, drawings, or second-hand garments. Photograph the outcome.

Fashion is about engaging with the world we are in and the people in it.

Fashion Relic

Go to a second-hand shop and select a garment that fits you. Put the garment on and imagine the person who wore this before you; pretend you are that person for 30 minutes.

Consider the following questions: Where did this person wear the garment? What types of actions did they perform in the garment? What other garments did they wear with it? What type of music did they listen to? Consider dancing to a song in the garment.

Record this process through film or photography.

Take the garment off. How do you feel? Record your thoughts/emotions in text in relation to the film and photographs.

Use this exercise to imagine and experience forgotten garments, old stock, garments gone out of fashion, fashion relics, and fashion memories. How can the experience of wearing someone else's discarded garment transcend your experience of time and place?

know your enemy

Recreate your foe's image with garments taken from private wardrobes. By recreating your enemy's style, you start to understand their motivations, feelings, and history up-close and personal.

Meet in a group of about four people. Have each person bring a big suitcase of personal belongings from their wardrobe (garments, accessories, makeup, and shoes).

Bring images of an enemy, or a group of people you have trouble understanding, etc.

Analyze what you see. Describe the bodies and physiognomy of your enemies. Look at their body surface and posture; describe their garments in detail; define the space and setting around them.

Start to decode the meaning of these components: What emotions, memories, references do they evoke?
Note your observations.

Use these notes to recreate your enemy's style through your wardrobe. Help each other create the perfect enemy look.

Compare your recreation with the printed images of your enemies. Do you look alike? Analyze the similarities and differences.

Share how you feel in your enemy's look.

writing from a garment's perspective

Pick a garment or pair of shoes from your closet.

Write a profile of this piece.

You can use the following questions (or make up your own):

What is this piece's name, gender, and age?
Where and when was it born?
Does it have siblings, lovers, mothers, fathers?
Is it happy?
Does it have any regrets?
What is this piece most proud of?
What are its goals in life?
What choices did this piece make in life?
Were these life changing and if so, how?

Take your time writing this profile. You can make it fictional, non-fictional (by researching the history of the piece), or a combination of both.

Write a short passage about moving to a new place from the perspective of the garment or pair of shoes. Be precise and pick your words carefully. When in doubt, ask yourself: Is this really a word the piece would use?

Consider using the profile for an entire collection of pieces in order to find its collective voice and story.

Getting to know your work is the most fun but also the most difficult part of being a maker. Writing about it can be hard. This exercise prompts you to take another perspective and find joy in writing about your work.

ways of (re-) collecting

If you are outside, go inside. If you are inside, go outside. Find a place where you can sit comfortably and (preferably) undisturbed.

Recollect a memory that you are very fond of.

Take as much time as you need; sit in the silence of your solitude and allow yourself the comfort (or perhaps discomfort) of your memories.

Resist the urge to name and place what you can recall. Instead, allow yourself to be consumed by the sweet sense of the moment.

Feel the weight of the words you cannot say, the smell you cannot name, the site you cannot place.

Translate this network of information into a shape.

Hold the memory of this shape in your mind until you are able to note it down.

Once you have noted this shape down, repeat it, interpret it, turn it inside out and upside down until you have enough shapes to put together.

(You may scale the shape on pattern paper; you may collect the shapes and fashion a zine; you may do with the shapes as you please.)

Extend this instruction to a friend and when you do, make sure to share your shape with them too.

You can whisper your shape into their ear like a secret; you can draw it in the sand, on a greasy napkin, in a notebook.

Collect as many shape-things as you can.

ridicule fashion manners

Try openly to attract public attention by the way you dress.
- Adopt a ridiculous, out-of-current-fashion style.
- Wear an outmoded and odd-coloured, odd-material garment.
- Wear the same garment every day for a month.
- Wear a design that ridicules dress codes.
- Use the wrong garments in or for the wrong situations.

In general Cato esteemed the customs and manners of men at that time so corrupt, and a reformation in them so necessary, that he thought it requisite, in many things, to go contrary to the ordinary way of the world. Seeing the lightest and gayest purple was then most in fashion, he would always wear that which was the nearest black; and he would often go out of doors, after his morning meal, without either shoes or tunic; not that he sought vain-glory from such novelties, but he would accustom himself to be ashamed only of what deserves shame, and to despise all other sorts of disgrace.[1]

This exercise deals with shame and garments. Accustom yourself to being ashamed only of what deserves shame and to rejecting all other forms of disgrace associated with being 'out of fashion'.

1   Plutarch, *Plutarch's Lives*, Volume 2 (New York: Modern Library Classics, 2001), 376.

not-making

1. Think about ways in which fashion design fosters and promotes the growth of the fashion industry and consumption of products. Write down a list of all the conscious or unconscious strategies you can think of (for example, fast-paced trends, cheap and poor quality manufacturing, cultural appropriation, etc.).

2. Pick one strategy.

3. Try to imagine the exact opposite strategy (for example, fast-paced trends versus one style forever).

4. Collect and/or invent strategies to make the opposite happen.

5. Pick one of these strategies.

6. Consider ways in which your concept could be (ab)used to make a profit and could cause any type of growth.

7. Present your findings (write, talk, visualize, collect, display, perform, etc.) ensuring no new fashion craze/mode/rage emerges.

8. Repeat steps 3 to 8 ad infinitum.

Capitalism continually threatens to disarm all of our alternative strategies, activisms, and criticisms by successfully assimilating them into narratives of profitable innovation and limitless growth. This is an exercise in imagining a radical way out of that conundrum. It is the ultimate (possibly futile) refusal.

anti-engagement strategy

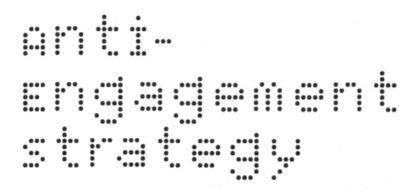

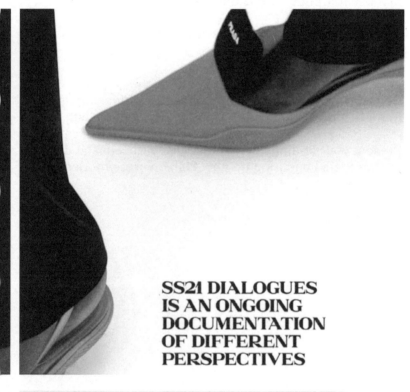

SS21 DIALOGUES IS AN ONGOING DOCUMENTATION OF DIFFERENT PERSPECTIVES

Maximilian Kilworth
@MaxKilworth

If tomatoes are a fruit then isn't ketchup a smoothie?
Answer at prada.com

2:00 AM · Jan 6, 2021

♡ 76   ◯   ⬆ Share this Tweet

D') YOUR
OI NT OF VIEW

1. Choose a brand that has a strong online presence.

2. Analyze the brand's language, both textual and visual. Evaluate the brand's values and its targeted audience. Create a map based on text and images captured from the brand's content. Pay specific attention to the ways in which you are being approached as a consumer. What is the brand's tone of voice? In what ways does this brand distinguish itself from others? What makes it special?

3. Create a visual and/or text-based expression using only existing material in a form that would repel the targeted audience. Think of ways to remix or distort the original content you have gathered during step two.

4. Give your anti-strategy a title and a byline and present your work online.

Digital fashion media and its branding and commerce create a continual and exhausting state of online engagement for consumers. In this exercise you will create a subversive engagement strategy by analyzing and reviewing the digital media you experience on a day-to-day basis. Subversive artistic strategies often distort or exaggerate existing things. Distortion intentionally confuses the 'fake and real' in order to pose provocative questions.

fashion fictions

This exercise invites you to imagine and describe a fictional fashion system in a parallel world where people live differently with their garments. It works well individually but can also be carried out in a small group.

1. Identify a specific issue relating to our real-world fashion system that frustrates you. Consider how this issue could be reversed to create a positive fashion system. (Alternatively, skip this step and work directly with a focused idea of a positive fictional fashion system).
   Describe your fictional fashion system. Your description should:
   - describe a contemporary reality in a parallel world (not the future in our world);
   - explore a positive and enticing culture in terms of individual satisfaction, social justice, and sustainability;
   - focus on use rather than production;
   - be physically possible but push beyond what feels plausible in our world.

2. Develop your core idea—the essence of your parallel world— by thinking in detail about a 'what if' question driving your fictional fashion system. Consider the location and scale of the fiction in the parallel world: is it local or global, niche or mainstream? Be playful as you imagine your world. Include quirky elements to make it memorable.

3. Generate a 'backstory' for your parallel world explaining why its fashion system developed differently to the system in our own world. Identify an event in history—genuine or invented—that caused the fictional world to split from our world. This event could have occurred months, years, or centuries ago.

4. Flesh out the idea and capture it in a one-hundred-word fiction piece. Use the first fifty words to describe the core idea and the backstory of your parallel world. Use the second fifty words to describe the everyday fashion practices in your world and the key aspects of its fashion culture.

body evolutions

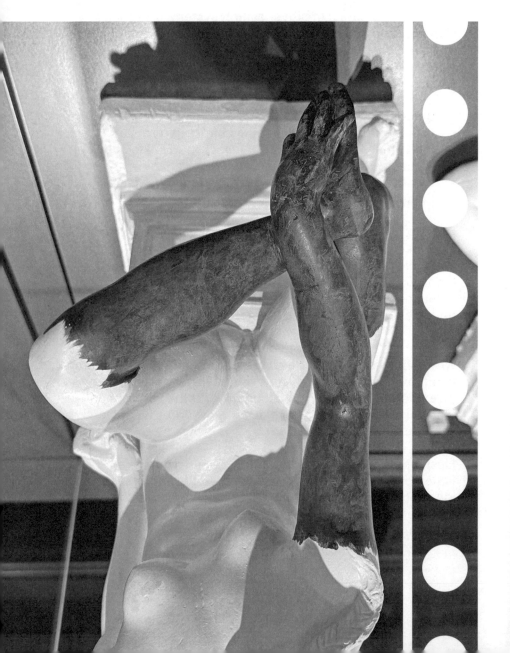

Imagine how the human body could evolve to prepare for the future.

Consider what abilities future bodies require. How do these abilities address current limitations, injustices, or imbalances in present day society? What senses could become amalgamated, enhanced, and added through these abilities? How might the skeletal and musculature elements of the body adapt? How would the mind, emotions, and body relate? What does this body look like? How does this body feel?

Capture your ideas through sketches, notes, collages, or a combination of all of these. Create three possibilities for future bodies.

Explore what these future bodies wear.

Consider the following questions: What does the body need from garments? How can garments aid bodily evolutions and adaptations? Explore different relationships between the body and garments (symbiotic, parasitic, functional, decorative).

Create at least three types of garments for the future bodies you developed.

The body evolves in response to material culture and its environment. Following the principles of posthumanism and transhumanism, some people augment bodily ability to identify as cyborgs rather than as humans. This speculative exercise imagines the possibilities of the future body in relation to garments.

interspecies collaborative design

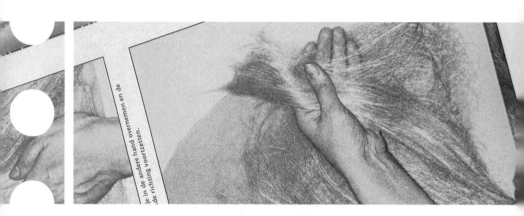

1. Determine who you will collaborate with.

The starting point for your interspecies design collaboration may be, for example, texture (leather-like kombucha or fluffy animal hair), organisms (work with something in the Plant Kingdom, rather than animals or insects), circularity (no waste is produced in the production and the product can return to its source after use), or outcome (a leather alternative or decorative surface design).

Some examples include:
- Algal plants who produce bioplastic.
- Fungi that produce foamy mycelium networks.
- Angora rabbits that produce long, luxurious hair.
- Insects that make scrappy cocoons from scraps of fabric.
- Bacteria that produce colourful stains on the surface of cloth.
- Kombucha SCOBYs that produce mats of leather-like bacterial cellulose.

A tree whose branches and roots can be formed into a basket to collect grasses to dye.

2. Research the chemical and biological conditions of the collaboration.

    Find design or scientific precedents in the area you are interested in. Research what is required to set up a collaborative engagement. Gather supplies.

3. Consider the social and ethical conditions of the collaboration.

    This is an exercise in working in the space between 'making' and 'growing'. While it invites you to move beyond the traditional production paradigms of 'extraction' and 'processing' to harness the morphological potential of a nonhuman living being, you must consider that power dynamics are present. You are the designer who is creating the conditions for the collaboration to exist. You cannot gain consent from your collaborator.

    When does the shaping of a paper shirt, for example, begin? The shaping happens long before the patternmaker or designer decides how to cut the paper cloth and style it. The shaping begins in the trees that produce the fibres for the shirt. Just as the potter's clay comes from sediments shaped eons ago, the paper shirt-maker's paper is shaped by processes that are just as old and just as embedded in a landscape as clay (e.g., weather, climate, groundwater, human care, etc.). The maker takes a position as nurturer of the material—coaxing it out of its original location—in a negotiational, sympoietic process of nurture and exchange.

The relationship between cultural and natural worlds is changing. Nature is no longer a background, something distant, or 'outside'. A figure of a more entangled world is emerging in which reciprocal forces between 'human-man', 'synthetic', and 'natural' push and pull. With this change, new methods of producing materials and form have emerged that are the product of complex relationships with nonhuman collaborators.

　　This exercise is an invitation to think radically about alternatives for design; it opens the door to new paradigms for interspecies collaboration. What can emerge in the nurturing, reciprocal space between 'making' and 'growing'?

A spell to Empower Independent Fashion Designers or collectives

You will need:
A handful of dried rose petals.
A handful of dried lavender.
Several drops of Jojoba oil.
A vanilla pod.
One pinch of ground cinnamon.
One charcoal disc.
One green candle.
One USB including written statements of new strategies for empowerment from each designer of the collective.

Blend the lavender, Jojoba oil, vanilla, and ground cinnamon and stir in a clockwise direction.

Light up the charcoal disc and add to it the blended mixture. Carve a word that represents your statement on the candle.

Hold the candle over the smoke; as you do this, imagine a goal you aim for as a young designer.

Place the rose petals around the candle and relight the candle every night for the next seven days; each time you do this, think about what you would like to represent as a designer or collective.

After you are done, store everything in a dark place inside your closet.

This spell aims to reverse the poisonous forces that systems of validation and power have over independent creatives in the fashion world. By empowering independent fashion designers or collectives—practices defined by aesthetic appreciation and critical reflexivity—it opens up a space for slowing down and rethinking strategies of acknowledging fashion.

a spell to slow down time

Take a pair of scissors outside on a warm night.

Follow the moonlight towards a supermarket that is an hour's distance from your house.

Go to the seeds section and buy some dill seeds. Sprinkle them under your pillow and next to your bare skin.

At this point the clearance of evil spirits and negative influences will begin.

To slow down time, collect jasmine leaves to activate the unheard sounds of dreams.

Let them dry on a full moon night.

Burn them in your bedroom using a long orange candle that reminds you of sunsets.

Look at the burning flame and think about what you value in fashion and how you can express this in a sustainable manner.

Nothing lasts forever as the fast-growing model of fast fashion quickly moves from season to season. This spell invites you to slow down time and potentially reverse the curse of mass production and constant need of consumption, while creating space for rethinking value in fashion.

Focus on the feeling of the cruel totality of capitalism and your own need to consume.

going outside

Fashion is intimate and personal, yet at its core it is a shared and public phenomenon—fashion is on the body, in architecture, and the objects around us. The exercises in 'Going Outside' encourage just that—to simply go outside. As our experience of the world becomes increasingly digital and oftentimes disconnected from physical, material fashion, especially in recent years, it is more important than ever to develop fashion design methods that are phenomenological. In other words, these exercises encourage you to source information through your direct experience of the real world.

The first thing you do when you go outside is notice. Notice the temperature, the way people are dressed, whether or not you wore the right shoes. In this theme, Kate Fletcher's 'Radical Noticing' and Daphne Mohajer va Pesaran's 'Intentional Noticing' ask you to bring rigor to the practice of noticing deeply and intentionally. What you document then becomes the raw material for your own ideas and anchor points to the world. Ferdinand Waas takes this one step further and asks you to then input what you noticed into the internet and go down the rabbit hole.

Developing an ability to notice can provide a foundation for radical subversion of fashion's institutions and systems. In 'Counter-Choreography', Aïcha Abbadi invites you to attend and study a fashion presentation and then stage an intervention via copying, parodying, and visualizing subtle subversions in real time. Alessandra Vaccari and Marco Marino ask you to 'spend time' instead of 'spending money' by closely observing a luxury fashion retailer and critically dissecting the subtle decisions made. In action, you start to see the invisible, seemingly immutable lines between 'luxury' and 'everyday' fashion. In the exercise 'G.U.C.C.I', Abigail Glaum-Lathbury also asks you to visit a luxury retailer, but is more direct in her approach: rather than simply noticing, she asks you to take something from the brand—a photo—to create a knockoff, subverting the power and immutability of luxury institutions.

Direct action has a place in radical fashion practice. It is a form of protest that is effective physically and

immediately, rather than depending
on negotiation and slow institutional
change. Mikhail Rojkov responds to
Audre Lorde's provocation that 'the
master's tools will never dismantle
the master's house' by inviting you to
produce 'counter-tools'. This exercise
approaches this by literally dismantling
an object, reverse-engineering it,
creating instructions, and placing it
back in the retailer from which it was
purchased. Direct action is a way to
create immediate effect and to connect
people, too. Otto von Busch's 'Pockets
for Peace' exemplifies this by asking you
to create pockets for specific objects
that give you a 'superpower'—the power
to immediately help others in a time
of need.

intentional Noticing

Decide a guiding question or intention—for example, what is casual dress? How do people wear accessories? How do people dress to fit into the city? Are gender assignments still important in dress? How do people dress their dogs? How do people in my city tend to sit in public? How do retail shops tell stories about fashion using imagery? What gestures do people make when they walk?

Select a destination that relates to your inquiry that is comfortable to sit or stand in for a long time.

Phone is off, on airplane mode, or somewhere else.

Settle in. Breathe deeply. Disappear and observe.

Start making rough 'scratch notes' (quick doodles, keywords, and phrases) and recordings (drawings, video, photographs, audio recordings, mental notes, poetic and descriptive text, anything). Let your mind wander and collect as much as you can in order to jog your mind later.

Be messy. Be patient. Follow your empathy and curiosity. Force yourself to sit in one spot for thirty minutes.

It will be boring, then it will be hard, then easy and exciting. You will get distracted. That is good. Don't use your phone. If you want to look something up, take note and do it later.

Go to another location. Repeat.

Back in the studio, revisit your rough notes and images right away. Enrich these 'scratch notes' to develop 'field notes'. These should be as detailed as possible and ideally be developed from the scratch notes on the same day as they were made.

When writing your field notes, you may want to use Dumit (2014) to ask questions.

This exercise encourages you to stop reading the world through screens and to go outside and gather first-hand documentation based on your experience of the real world. You will then translate this into your own creative language, whether it be material, text, or other forms of fashion expression.
    This process is not about editing—this is only about generating.

Note: This exercise was conceived as part of the
    Master of Fashion (Design) curriculum in the
    School of Fashion and Textiles at RMIT
    University, Melbourne.

radical
Noticing

- Locate your body. Bring yourself out of your head and whatever fashion look or moment you are experiencing and find your limbs, your breath, your skin.

- Extend your senses further than your body. What is it like where you are? Who is with you? Can you see the sky? What colour is the most dominant in your surroundings?

- Locate the body-garment sensations. What do you feel? How does your garment shape you? What does it enable you to do?

- Move. Walk, run, climb a ladder, a flight of stairs, a hill. What happens then? What do you notice about the world? And your clothed body?

- Use the process of radical noticing to make a change. How do you design fashion differently now? How do your research questions change?

This activity cultivates the practice of 'noticing' our lived experience of a garment—its relationship to the body and the world—to promote awareness, care, connection, responsibility, and action. Noticing is akin to appreciation. Noticing develops our understanding of how a garment is made, what it can do, how it can be worn, washed, worn again, repaired. But noticing is like a muscle. We need to flex it, work it, enjoy the power it gives us. Noticing is the first step in a bigger journey of valuing and satisfaction across many parts of our lives. It helps see our lives as tangled together—me and this garment—as part of the same life. This makes noticing a political act. It is about how we choose to live.

Notes on globalized fashion

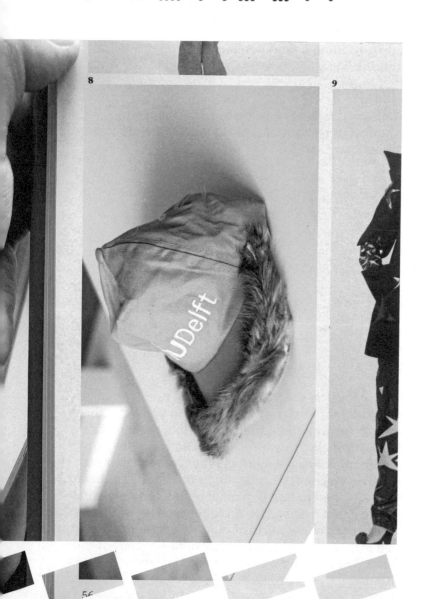

Let's start with observation.

Choose a semi-busy street and observe what people are wearing.

Note any repetition in the garments you observe. What type of garment pieces are popular?

Write a list (on your phone or in a notebook) of these garments.

Choose one that you feel personally intrigued by.

On the way back home reflect on your connections to this garment.

Once home, on your computer, open an internet search engine.

Search for the staple garment. Follow hyperlinks, new tab, new tab, until you have at least ten to fifteen tabs open.

Now start reading, keeping in mind what you just saw on the street.

Engage with the historical detail, anecdotes, stories, paintings, notes, documents, and archives of the garment you are researching.

Find a story about the garment that you can share with your friends as a 'random fact'. For example, 'By the way, yesterday I read…'

Design or conceive a new garment based on your 'random fact'. Take this research literally in your design. Tell the historical story through the garment staple, tell the garment staple through the historical story.

counter-choreography

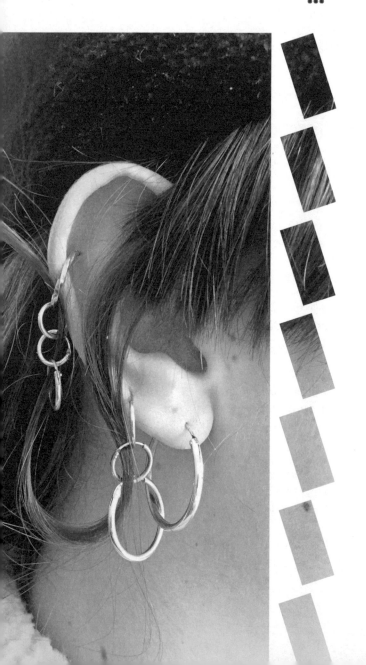

Check your local area for upcoming fashion events. Find a co-conspirator and pick a setting.

Write a list of the particular norms of this setting: the space, the characters, the language used in this context, the rules for interaction, invisible actors involved (for example, marketing teams, technical staff, guest list curators) and the role you are expected to play.

Let your outfit be either:
- a parody of what you would usually wear;
- a reference to the venue's historical or political context;
- a visualization of the 'elephant in the room': a topic that remains unaddressed or for which the event acts as a smokescreen;
- a replica of one of the uniforms event staff are wearing (think: security, catering, drivers, etc.).

In your interactions at the event, decide whether to:
- appear as a pair, i.e. for staged conversations;
- separate for simultaneous actions and parallel narratives;
- involve more guests one by one until the event plays out in several layers.

Think of a role and behave accordingly. The role can but does not need to match your outfit. Examples include:
- Inversion: someone who represents the exact opposite of the role you are expected to play, the reason you were invited. (This role brings attention to cliques and homogeneous opinions, incorporating dissent and debate).
- Time traveller: someone who used the venue in the past, such as a factory worker, or aristocrat. (This role brings attention to shifts in power and questions ownership past and present).
- Backstage: host, technical team, etc. (This role brings attention to the effort behind the scenes and the artifice of the event).

This activity helps fashion practitioners develop a set of expressions and behaviours that act as a counter-weight to learned social choreographies in professional settings. Conscious counter-movement highlights the strangeness of fashion's conventions and rituals, questioning them in order to find new meaning and purpose in everyday actions.

spending
time

Leave home.

Go to the main shopping street of your city.

With your eyes, take possession of the area.

Choose as a case study a fashion retail space that you usually avoid entering because it is too expensive or too 'high fashion'. It could be a luxury brand shop or a multi-brand retailer.

Consider the display system and the brand's strategies inside or outside of its premises.

Focus on the visual and sensorial elements that initially strike your attention. Identify an object/subject of interest for your exercise. For instance: windows, garments, accessories, furniture, lights, shop assistants, scent, shopping bags, or textiles. Does your chosen element arouse your interest, fear or humour?

In response, make phone notes using drawings, photos, poetry, and creative and uncreative writing. You can either appropriate the chosen element (embrace the idea) or re-programme it as an ironic gesture.

'Spending time' instead of 'spending money' invites you to have the luxury of time and to rethink the role of luxury in our culture. Pay attention to, and critically dissect, the elements and values that high fashion retailers are selling you. Play with these elements and be responsive to your surroundings.

G.U.C.C.I. (genuine unauthorized clothing clone institute)

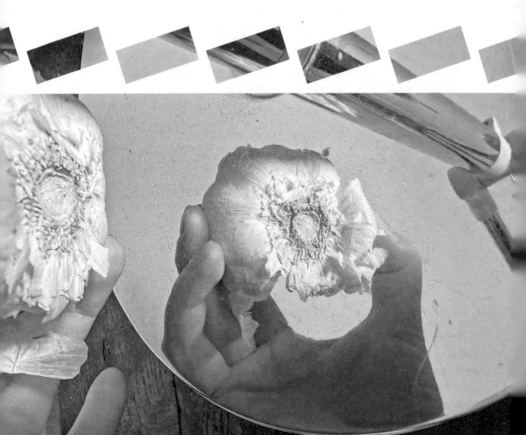

Abigail Glaum-Lathbury · G.U.C.C.I. (Genuine Unauthorized
       Clothing Clone Institute)

1. Find a store that carries brands from luxury conglomerates
    (for example, LVMH Louis Vuitton Moët Hennessey,
    Richemont, Kering, etc.).

2. Select a garment from the shop floor to try on in the
    dressing room and take a selfie in it.

3. Transfer the selfie image to your computer and remove the
    background so that only the silhouette of your body in the
    garment remains.

4. Make a list of:
    ▪   The things that make the garment interesting to you.
    ▪   How the garment made you feel.
    ▪   The things you wish the garment had and ways that the
        garment could make you feel different.

5. Use the mirror selfie as the basis for a new and improved
    garment based on your list of desires.

6. Create a new logo.

7. Brand your new design with your new logo and submit for
    copyright protection.

Advances in technology have transformed fashion: not only
in the way that garments are produced, but also in the way
that they are consumed. Fashion is on the precipice of a
post material world—we now consume fashion through the
flattened screens of our telephones and tablets. The distinction/
conformity polarity is now performed through images and the
curated feeds of Instagram. The impermanent and continually
shifting desire to both stand out and blend in has accelerated
to a rate just faster than the speed of production itself. Luxury
fashion houses have long ceased to make truly distinctive
garments, opting instead to monetize ubiquity through
trademarked logos. This exercise invites you to challenge this
practice by producing clones of luxury items.

counter-tools

1. Get a seam ripper, a camera, and a transparent resealable (bio)plastic bag.

2. Go to a garment shop.

3. Choose a garment you like.

4. Pay for it. You can also steal a garment, but this is not recommended.

5. Leave the shop and go to a place where you feel comfortable. Here you will start a labour of care.

6. Get out your seam ripper and your camera.

7. Deconstruct the purchased garment and take pictures of all the steps in the process. Take care to unstitch each seam without rushing.

8. Once the garment is completely deconstructed, carefully iron all the pieces flat. Remove any thread ends that remains on the pieces at the seams. Sort the pieces by size and material.

9. Put them in the resealable (bio)plastic bag and label the bag.

10. Collect all the pictures taken during deconstruction, reverse the order of disassembly to recreate the order of assembly and put them together to form a user manual. You can use an IKEA furniture assembly instruction manual as a guide.

11. Print the manual and insert it in your resealable bag. Close it.

12. Take your kit back to the shop where you bought your garment and find, if possible, the shelf where the garments like the one you bought are hanging.

13. Find a free hanger and hang your kit on the front of the shelf.

14. Observe.

What if Audre Lorde* was right? What if 'the master's tools will never dismantle the master's house'? What counter-tools could dismantle it? If we consider the needle as the fashion master's tool, is the seam ripper the ultimate counter-tool?

*   Audre Lorde (1934–1992) was a black American lesbian feminist writer. In 1984, Lorde wrote the influential text 'The Master's Tools Will Never Dismantle the Master's House.' The essay contends that anyone can be the oppressor (master) of someone who has less privilege and, further, that those who built our contemporary society (house) cannot be removed from their dominant position using the tools (oppression) upon which they built it.

rockets for peace

1. Think of a superhero: What is their special power? How do they use it? Can you have a superpower? What would your superpower be?

2. Think of everyday objects and their powers. What kind of objects do you carry with you every day? Or on special occasions? What do they enable you to do? (For instance, keys enable you to open specific doors. A snack raises your blood sugar level. A screwdriver enables you to operate screws. Needle and thread help you repair garments).

3. Focus on the objects that you can share with others or use together: Can you use these objects with the purpose of promoting peace? (Can you share your snack to energize someone who is in need? Can you help repair a stranger's stroller with the screwdriver? Can you use your needle and thread to darn a hole in your friend's garments?).

4. Choose the object or tool you are most comfortable with. Make a special pocket for this object on the inside of your garment to make sure you always carry your hidden superpower. Have your power available and ready to share at all times.

5. Practice your new superpower. Try to recognize where you can intervene. Change your focus of attention; the world is always in need of your power, your care, and of repair.

6. Use the pocket to promote peace.

The aim of this exercise is to explore the capacity for change in everyday objects and how making special pockets for such objects can shift our attention and agency in the world.

The body is always the starting point for fashion. From the fleshy body that wears it, to the rigid, standardized sizing systems that are used to design for it.

Fashion also has a habit of excluding and idealizing bodies via the trope of the mannequin. In 'Impossible Armatures', Matthew Linde rethinks the mannequin—the ultimate symbol of fashion standardization—as a pillar of fashion exhibition-making. Paola Di Trocchio's 'Body Exhibition' goes even further by making our bodies the site of the exhibition entirely.

Sanem Odabaşı's exercise, 'Unpacking the Memory of Garments', eliminates sight altogether, using textual description to encounter fashion. We also see an exploration of the haptic dimensions of fashion in Silvia Bombardini's 'Haptic Experience', which asks us to encounter the 'underbelly, soft insides, and prickly labels' of our garments by turning our wardrobe inside out. Vidmina Stasiulytė's 'Sound to Wear' and PAGEANT's 'Soundscape of a Look' also forgo sight to explore the aural dimensions of garments.

On the most basic level, fashion is

continually performed by the body
that wears it. Todd Robinson, Linnea
Bågander, and Laura Banfield each look
at the moving, performing body as a
starting point for design. Bågander's
exercise, 'Designing from Movement',
for instance, explores the 'aesthetic
potential and somatic experience of
material'. The radicality of these exercises is to foreground the body, rather
than the aesthetic of garments, as an
experimental and generative tool for
design.

impossible armatures

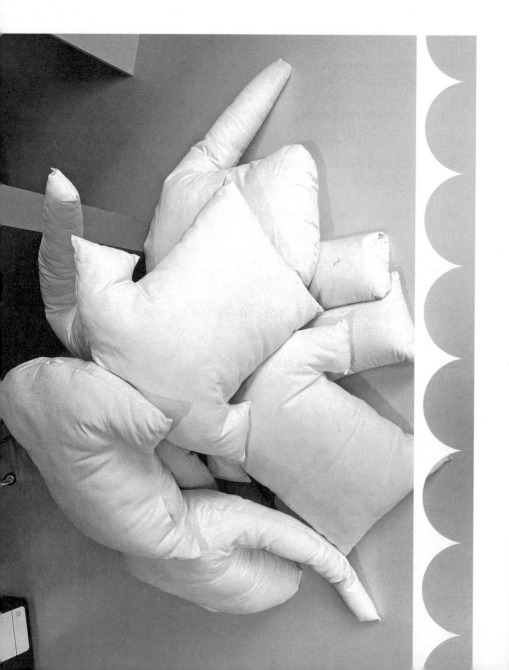

This exercise embraces the impossibility of the body in exhibiting fashion.

Task: test new surrogate bodies and armatures to mount your garment. Reflect on how these generate novel psychological and morphological narratives with the garment.

Try mounting your garment on furniture—chairs, tables, hat stands, lamps—and found materials—rope, branches, tape, cardboard— to create abstract mannequins and humanoid figures.

Or why not try other, non-human animals? Consider squeezing, compressing, and concealing it between crevices and objects. Ignore inflating the garment with the body altogether—suspend, lay, scrunch. Use wadding to engorge, swell, and pressurize.

How do armatures reanimate garments and their narratives?

The disjuncture between body and dress haunts the fashion exhibition. Dress, no longer enlivened by the fleshy, moving body, is mounted on armatures that gesture at us, that mime a lost corporeality.

body
exhibition

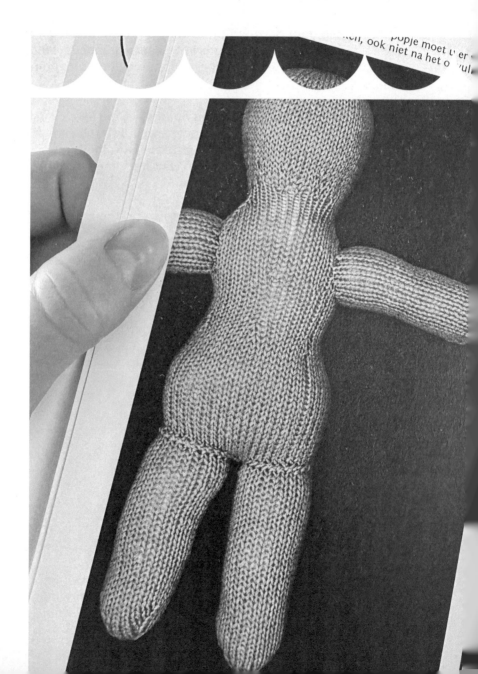

Popje moet t' er ... en, ook niet na het o ... vul

1. Select a fashion object (historical or contemporary).

2. Research the historical and cultural meaning and context of your object. Research the historical and cultural meaning and context of your object. Use the material culture methodology to interpret the object following a four-step process of description, deduction, speculation, and evaluation (Steele 1998).[1]

3. Combine the object with other fashion objects from different historical periods and/or designers to create an ensemble that reflects your chosen theme.

4. Compose an ensemble on your body with your collection of objects. If you are doing this conceptually, represent the ensemble through illustration (digital or otherwise).

5. Name your body exhibition.

6. Write a one to two hundred word didactic text explaining your body exhibition.

7. Place your body exhibition in an environment and record it with images or film.

Fashion writer Anna Piaggi (1931–2012) was often referred to as a 'walking museum' in her curatorial approach to dressing. This exercise explores the concept of the 'walking museum' and how fashion objects can be embodied in select combinations to perform exhibitions on the body. It can be undertaken as a conceptual exercise since museum collections and/or historic items may be difficult to acquire.

1   In particular, this method extracts information from mute objects through *description* (observing and recording the physical characteristics of the object); *deduction* (recognize, acknowledge, and test assumptions of the perceiver on the object); *speculation* (assessing the object against external questions and hypotheses using external evidence and resolution); and finally, *evaluation*, which presents a judgement or position. Using this methodology, interpret a theme or concept from the object.

covering

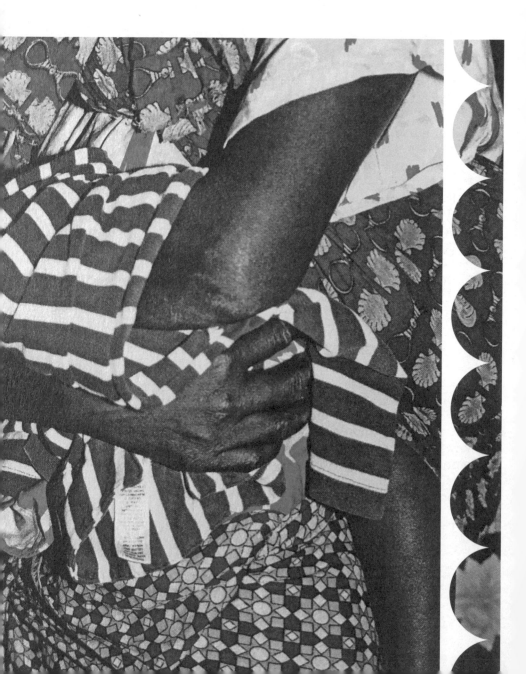

This exercise aims to expand the notion of the body by seeing objects without bodily qualities as entities with latent potential to be fashion bodies. The act of covering presents an opening, a new surface on which to intervene, to comment, to communicate.

1. Start with a body. This could be your own body, someone else's body, a representation of a body (sculpture/image), or an object that may have bodily attributes (including an object without bodily qualities where you might see a potential to 'make it' a body).

2. Document the 'body' photographically, scan digitally, or capture it on film. Document all angles, front to back, top to bottom.

3. Select the image/screengrab where you see the most potential.

4. Print the image in a medium of your choosing: on paper, fabric, or other (the scale should be in relation to the original object or could challenge the scale in different ways).

5. Return the image back to the original object/body. Paste, affix, hang, place, fold, and drape to explore the new relation between object/body/image and material.

What have you created? A new abstract garment, a visual interpretation of a new body, a wearable form, a dialogue between object and image? Or image and body? What does it communicate now? What potential do you see for further development?

Head garnish

判断のつかないグレー・ゾーンを生み出している。

●TWA Transit
エーロ・サーリ
ケネディ空港の
なレプリカを帽
洋服も当時のTW
帽子・ヘルメッ
ると、多くの人

の顔が
込む
乗り換え(トラン
のツール

Your upcoming Costume Institute retrospective will feature your work across an impressive armada of mannequins. Regrettably, the Institute's remaining budget has been drained by a malicious cyberattack, bereaving the mannequins of any wigs or headpieces. Adding insult to injury, the entire banking system has been shut down, severing you from global trade. All you have to remedy the situation are those everyday materials that are readily available.

This exercise activates the mannequin via its headpiece. You will experiment how a mannequin headpiece made of a single material motif can represent your collection/body of work.

Use one DIY/ad-hoc material to envision your own simple headpiece that will adorn an imaginary mass of mannequins wearing your designs in a speculative major exhibition.

The material motif must be cohesive and budget conscious. Experiment with how simple material gestures, much like the gesture of a sketch, can represent your design spirit. Consider how the headpiece garnishes your work as a complete whole.

If you don't have a foam head, you can use a head-shaped object like a large bowl for your mount. You can also use a basic fixture (such as tape or pins) to secure and shape the material.

Consider: cling wrap, rubber, fine chain, boxes, paper, kitchen utensils, furniture, rope, carpet, foam, plant matter, bottles, glass, string, fabric, dust, aluminium, wood, dollar store wigs, tinsel, bags, or any object that is found in aggregate. Be as excessive or sparing, unkempt or delicate as you desire.

jewellery Hunting

Notice when light and shadow produce a fleeting moment of beauty.

Place yourself in the light, letting it fall on your body to create immaterial jewellery.

Capture it with a photograph.

'Jewellery Hunting' invites participants to hunt for a beautiful effect of light, wear it as jewellery, and capture it. Visualizing the sensation of wearing jewellery in this manner highlights the possibility of jewellery being immaterial. The aim is to make people aware of new values based on experimental personal aesthetics.

Design for moving bodies

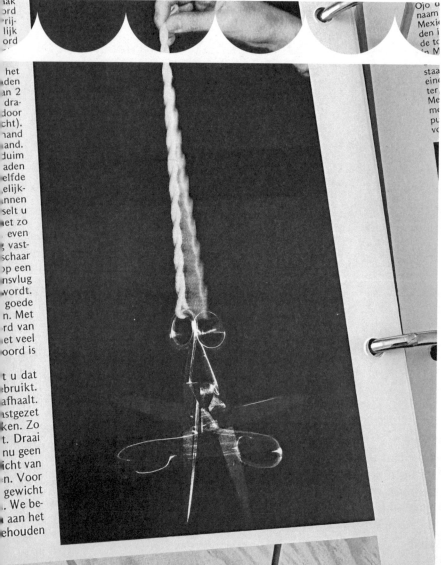

1. Explore several garments in your wardrobe. Consider them in terms of the criteria: material, form, and relationship to the body. Some garments might be long, others short, some tight, some loose, some crisp, some slack, some may be snug or slim fit, while others might produce a sense of space and freedom in their relationship to the body. They will relate to and contact the body in different ways and places.

2. Try the garments on, integrating them into ensembles that please you, one by one. Don't look at yourself in the mirror. Go for a walk, sit, stand, turn, stretch, dance, and move. Explore the different bodily sensations these garments produce and the feelings, movements, and thoughts that you associate with them.

3. Trace connections between the properties of the garments and those sensations. Write these down, along with descriptions of the movement qualities they produce, into a 'Movement Glossary'.

4. Drawing on your insights gathered in your Movement Glossary, identify a series of words you can use as a catalyst for design. Choose two as a minimum, with three or four as a maximum. These words should be associated with movement and should be descriptive. For example, perhaps you felt 'active, lively, sporty' while in another garment you felt 'languid, fluid, and side-to-side', yet in another 'brisk, simplified, and direct'. Use your movement words as a starting point to design and construct a new outfit. You can use any colour, material, or technique to do this. When designing its shape, form, and material, imagine yourself wearing the garment and the kinds of physical sensations, thoughts, and feelings that it might produce.

This exercise reflects on the relationship between garments and the moving body by acknowledging that fashion's influence on how we feel shapes how we move. The focus for you, as the designer, is not to design garments that, for example, look 'languid', but rather to design something to produce the feeling of being languid. Designing for the moving body shifts the focus beyond thinking of fashion exclusively in terms of visual appearances and aesthetics.

The intersection of body and material

Image: Laura Banfield
Performer: Deanne Butterworth
From 'The Intersection of Body & Material' class led

1. Select several garments from your wardrobe. Consider their shape, size, material characteristics, and what might make for some interesting and varied experiments. Anything goes!

2. Think of your garments as objects and brainstorm all the different ways that, in an instant, your body can manipulate them. Use action words (such as twist, pull, and drop) as prompts.

3. Choose one of these actions and test it out on a garment. Try doing it to different parts of the garment.

4. Expand your choreography by changing how you perform the action. For example, make the action bigger, smaller, faster, slower, higher, lower, louder, quieter.

5. Try using different body parts to perform the same action on your garments. If it feels silly, you're doing it right! Be experimental. For example, try pants on your arm, or a shirt upside-down. Continue exploring your choreography as before.

6. Bring a piece of furniture, prop, or another body into the mise en scène. Consider attaching your garment to it and test out your choreography. Can you shift your intention so that it is your garments, instead, that help apply the action to your body? Or can both perform the action simultaneously? What additional elements might you need to achieve this?

7. Take note of any interesting discoveries. Was there an interplay of light or sound? Did you explore the movement of your body, garment, or both in unexpected ways? How was movement enhanced or hindered? In what ways could you elevate the performance?

8. Repeat and expand your most successful experiments into concepts for garments, costume, and performance.

Fashion design typically begins with a sketch, pattern, or mannequin. However, our bodies are not as static as these forms dictate. This exercise explores the collaboration between a moving body and its garments as a premise for design.

Designing from move‑ment

1. Explore a part of the body and its movement. The hand is a good place to start since it can do many different movements. What movements can the body part perform? What do you find interesting about these movements? Document with film and extract still images from key points.

2. Choose one movement and explore at least three fabrics that express different interpretations of that movement (for example, stiff felted wool, soft flowy silk, rigid straws, elastic bands, fringe, etc.). When arranging the material on the body part, think about what key points need to be involved in the design in order to accentuate the movement (you can use a glove or pantyhose to pin the materials on the hand). Document with film and extract still images.

3. Develop the most interesting fabric into a final design. If there is time, scale it up to interact with the whole body.

This exercise explores design based on the movement of a performing body. The design outcome does not necessarily focus on designing for efficiency of movement but rather on the aesthetic potential and somatic experience of the moving body material.

unpacking
the memory
of garments

Start with a garment you own and think is special. Write your thoughts on why this garment is special.

Use your senses.

1. Taste: Does your garment have a taste? (For example, were you biting a piece of thread as a habit when you were studying, reading?) Write.

2. Vision: What is the shape and form of your garment? What are the details? What do you feel when you see them? Write.

3. Hearing: Does your garment have a sound when you touch it? What about when you wear it? Can others hear it too, or is it only for you? Write.

4. Smell: What kind of smell does your garment have? Which season are you wearing it in? Write.

5. Touch: What is the texture of the fabric? What kind of energy does it have? What is the mood of the fabric? Write.

Garments hold memories: a smell or a colour from our garments can unlock 'mnemonic energies' that fashion materials keep within them. Textiles, garments, and fabrics bear the traces of daily life and have the capacity to store stains, smells, and sweat. The aim of this method is to unpack the memories of garments by revealing their ability to stimulate memory.

the art studio of the mouth

1. Find a simple food you can eat. For example, an almond, a tomato, or a piece of bread. Put it in your mouth and chew thoroughly.

2. Reflect on what happens in your mouth. How do the textures feel? Describe the mouthfeel in at least twenty words (for example: chewy, grainy, oily, coarse, textured, drying, etc.).

3. Find five colours that best express the mouthfeel and give the colours names (for example: autumn grey, melancholic green, etc.).

4. Draw the mouthfeel. Is it dotty, uneven, or round? Use different pens and pencils to express your impressions in black and white sketches.

5. Combine colours and sketches into motifs and patterns. Make as many as you like.

6. Create a 'material buffet' with thirty different white materials with a variation in texture and tactility—from wool and paper to small stones and plastic. Find materials that relate to the mouthfeel (for example: natural, synthetic, soft, hard, crackling). Collect items from the buffet and arrange them on a piece of cardboard. It will result in a texture map or a landscape of textures.

7. If the mouthfeel was a person, how would that person be? Write a brief text from the textures' point of view (for example, the almond could be an old man).

   Now you have different elements you can combine. Ask yourself how you can transform these findings. Depending on what you eat, the outcome will be different. Try this with at least four different foods.

This exercise exposes the aesthetics behind mouthfeel and transforms it into a design methodology. Mouthfeel is the tactile sense of eating. It is the sensory characteristics that are materialized by the structural qualities of food. The aim of this activity is to present a methodology to translate these impressions to lasting expressions embodied in colour, materials, and texture.

soundscape of a look

96

1. Select at least one garment, one pair of shoes, and one accessory to use for your fashion field recording.

2. Find a quiet place—this could be in your actual wardrobe or room with a closable door.

3. Over the duration of three minutes, use your recording device (a smartphone or a microphone) to document the following:
   - Put the garment on, then take it off. Does it slip over the head, is there a zip or multiple buttons to do up?
   - Put the shoes on, then take them off. Do they slip on or do they have laces that need to be tied up?
   - Place the accessory on, then take it off. Does it go over the hand, wind through the fabric, or suspend on the body?

4. Listen back to the field recording. How would you describe the ambience of the three experiences of dressing? What is the distinctive character and expression of each sound?

5. Describe the sounds using six words.

6. Using the six words, draw them as individual shapes or colours.

7. Merge the six shapes or colours into three new hybrid combinations.

8. Use these combinations to form garment silhouettes or garment pattern pieces for the body for further development.

How does sound identify and define a sense of place on the body? How does sound create a sense of context for the wearer as an experience? This exercise documents the acoustic environments of 3D forms by recording a sequence of soundscapes from garments in your wardrobe.

sound to wear

Experiment 1
Collect various objects that are nearby.
Put each object close to your ear(s) and listen.
Alternate between the objects and explore while listening.
What sounds do you hear?
How does the object change the perceived sound?
You can do this sitting or standing.

Experiment 2
In a group, wear eye masks.
Choose a fabric that makes an interesting sound.
Play with it: touch it, fold and unfold it, wear it, sit on it, etc.
Stand in a circle with the other participants.
Perform as a group. Translate the sound using body
movements.
How are the rhythms and sounds connected?

Experiment 3
Select an object that you like the sound of.
Attach it to your arm(s).
Sound it.
Attach it to the gap between the inner side of your arm and
torso.
Sound it.
Attach it to your armpit(s).
Sound it.
Attach it between your legs.
Sound it.
Attach it to your buttock(s).
Sound it.
Attach it to your chest.
Sound it.
Attach it to your back.
Sound it.
Attach it to your elbow(s).
Sound it.
Attach it to any other place on your body and sound it.
What differences in sonic expression did you notice?
What movements did you use to make the object sound?

Experiment 4
Design a garment using different tempos.
Activate the garment such that it sounds.
What sonic expressions are you creating?
What movements did you use to activate the object?

Fashion is primarily a visual ontology consisting of definitions,
theory, and design methods that are based on visual language.
This set of experimental performative exercises critiques the
defining practices of fashion design and wear by finding ways
to include marginalized and differently-abled bodies within the
system of fashion.

sensuous description

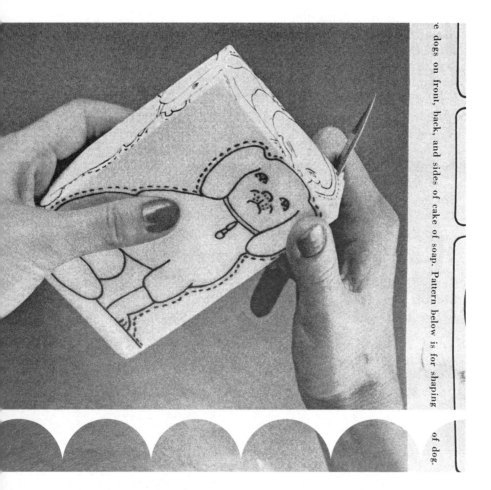

1. Select a wearable object.

2. Write or audio record a sensory description of the object without reference to visual characteristics or terms. A blindfold may be useful for focus. Think creatively about the words used to describe the object (similes, synaesthetic metaphors, invent your own words). Pay attention to any associated emotional responses throughout the process.

Prompts:
- Describe the soundtrack of wear or the 'voice' of the object. What sounds are made when the object is worn, held, manipulated, dropped?
- Note the olfactory characteristics and atmosphere (material, bodily, environmental). Imagine the object as a scent, for example, 'robust and hairy, with notes of whiskey and twenty-year-old polyester'.
- Feel the object with different parts of your body and notice the changes—fingertips, palm of hand, back of the hand, arms, stomach, and legs. How does feeling (touching) this object make you feel (emotionally)?

3. Edit these sensory notes into a description of the object. This is a sensuous (deep, lush, affective) description.

4. Based only on the description, design a new garment. It should not visually replicate the initial fashion object, but prompt new design enquiries based on the sensory characteristics discovered and identified through the descriptive process.

Variation 1:
- Do this activity with someone else.
- Use a blindfold; the other person will give you an object to describe.
- They will audio record your responses.
- Once the prompts are completed, remove the blindfold to see the object.
- Reflect on how seeing the object changed your perception of it.

Variation 2:
Give the final description of your object to another person as a design prompt, without them seeing the initial object. Compare the original object and new design to reflect on the sensory experience of fashion and its relationship to language.

The privileging of sight in the experience of fashion has dominated its language. This exercise explores sensuous description outside of visual terms as a method of sensory fashion practice.

Haptic experience

1. Turn all the garments in your wardrobe inside out. Their underbelly, soft insides, and prickly labels will be what you face when you open its doors.

2. Shift the hangers around until you forget their original position. Leave them there and go to sleep.

3. In the morning, don't turn the light on. Keep the blinds shut, the curtains drawn. Open your wardrobe and dress only by touch. Remember that what you are touching is the inside of garments, not what people will feel if they touch you—but rather what you feel on your bare skin. Think about your body in the day ahead. What does it want? For example: lightness, coolness, warmth, the tight embrace of lycra, the solid stiffness of denim, the audible swish of something beaded, to ground you in the present and in your movements, to make yourself heard?

'Why should our bodies end at the skin?' Donna Haraway asked in her 1991 text *Simians, Cyborgs, and Women: The Reinvention of Nature.* This exercise cultivates haptic pleasure in wearing garments, rejecting the objectifying gaze of the fashion industry and foregrounding how good a garment feels over how good it makes the wearer look. It aims to take the wearer one step closer to the fluid continuity with our garments that feminist thought invites us to pursue.

Collaboration and collectivity are essential to all fashion production. We need to explore more personal, meaningful, and non-hierarchical ways of working and making together to get to a more equitable system of fashion. Exercises in this theme use garments and fashion as personal exchange and as a way to communicate with each other.

For instance, Adele Varcoe's exercise 'Outfit Swap', which opens this section, asks of us the most intimate act of all: sharing another person's garments. Adele asks us to be someone else for a time, and invite them to be us, by swapping wardrobes with them, inhabiting their tops, bottoms, socks, shoes, and even underwear for the more bold reader. By doing so, we can learn about another's experience in the world, and their stories told through individual garments. To add to this, fashion collective PUGMENT looks at the social practices of doing laundry in Japan by asking us to do our laundry together and exchange stories about our garments in 'Laundry and Dialogue'.

Some exercises in this section embrace collective and communal making. Lenn Cox, Soft Baroque, and Johanna Tagada Hoffbeck's exercises look at where the authorship is shared through methods of collective making, and where the outcome can only exist because of collective, rather than individual, input. Soft Baroque's 'Body Objects', in which we are asked to collectively make through a relay-based format, distributes the authorship of an object among participants. These exercises flatten the hierarchies of production in ways that, if scaled up, could radically challenge fashion's system of authorship and even ownership.

Exercises in this theme also explore the tension between dressing as a personal, individual experience, and one that is also inherently shared with those around us (communities and friends both global and local). Udochi Nwogu gives us a method to experience and explore wearing together as a way of being together. In 'Fashion for Community', Nwogu explores the concept of *aso ebi* and shares a method for creating collective experiences of dressing among friends and family.

outfit swap

This exercise is an exploration of the feelings that arise when we swap the entire outfit that is on our body with another body's outfit. It is most effective when done spontaneously. No need to prepare. Jump in the deep end.

Find someone to swap your entire outfit with (including socks, underwear, shoes).

Decide together on the duration of the swap.

Observe and take notes of the way you feel before, during, and after the swap. Take notes on the interactions and conversations you have. Write down and perhaps sketch some of the experiences you have.

Reunite and share your experience.

Want to step it up?

Follow the steps above and swap your entire wardrobe for a minimum of one month.

*If this exercise sets off alarm bells, write down why. Sometimes the reasons why you won't do something can be just as revealing as the reasons why you would.

upside down pressing

1. Find someone to work with. This exercise works best in a group of at least two people.

2. Find some garments in your wardrobe that you are no longer interested in wearing and are happy to cut up. Find a top and a bottom at a second-hand shop that you wouldn't normally wear.

3. Cut the garments from your wardrobe into smaller pieces— for example, turn a single garment into two or three separate pieces.

4. Join the pieces to a top and a bottom from the second-hand shop. (You can use any method to join the pieces to garments, but think about their functionality, rather than their decoration).

5. Exchange your finished garments with others in the group.

6. As a group, explore ways of dressing these unfamiliar garment forms.

7. Document your way of dressing with photography and share with others in the group.

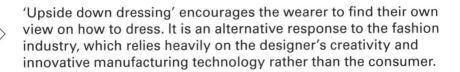

'Upside down dressing' encourages the wearer to find their own view on how to dress. It is an alternative response to the fashion industry, which relies heavily on the designer's creativity and innovative manufacturing technology rather than the consumer.

The intertextuality of collaboration

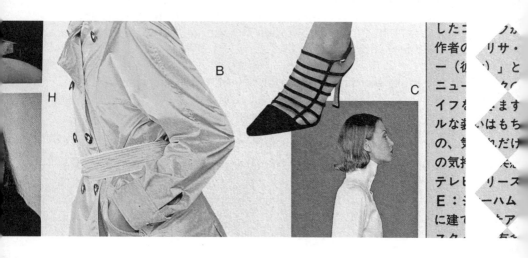

This is a group exercise designed for three to six participants.

First, the group collectively decides on a set of criteria. This may include as many of the following: a colour, a decade, a music track, a film or book, and/or a face (a known or unknown muse).These can be as low or highbrow, intellectual or humorous as your group decides. You are the designers and this is your cultural capital. You are creating your own paradigm.

An example of a set of criteria:
Colour: Red
Decade: 1940s
Music Track: 'Das Model' by Kraftwerk
Film: *The Devils* by Ken Russell
Face: Winona Ryder

These chosen elements will create the parameters for sourcing your category of garments. These words will be a recipe for your 'aesthetic world' and as a team you are responsible for creating this world through your sourced garment categories. Provide at least three options for each category.

Secondly, each participant brings in several garments from a chosen set of categories. These garments may be borrowed from a friend, bought at a second-hand store, or taken from participants' own wardrobes. Examples of categories include: trousers; dresses; outerwear; shirts; jersey; knitwear; shoes; handbags; accessories.

Thirdly, gather the following:
- A garment rail.
- A model of any gender and of any physical description— it's your world.
- A phone/camera to take photos.
- A space that will be a canvas for your fitting.

Finally, pool your findings and place the garments and accessories on the rail into looks. Document these on your model and keep moving pieces into different looks to create differing proportions and silhouettes. You could also think about looks as sisters/partners/multiples.

Print each of the looks. Now you have the start of a collaborative springboard to expand on and create stories within a collection. This is a map to understanding proportion, colour, texture, feel, weight, image, and movement for your season.

Teamwork and collaboration are essential parts of creating in-depth multi layered fashion collections. But how does each designer find their voice within a team of strong individuals? This exercise dissolves hierarchy in a design studio team by requiring each member to contribute equally in the creative process. It facilitates an understanding of how research and design ideas can be interpreted through existing fashion objects, and how a 'studio team' approaches collections collaboratively.

body objects

You will need:

- One big table in the studio or outside.
- One hot glue gun.
- Air dry clay.
- A variety of studio materials at hand (offcuts, paper, wire, threads, cloth, etc.).
- A variety of natural materials if performing outside (sticks, rocks, etc.).

Materials can be collectively selected/harvested by participants and/or prepared by the conductor prior to the exercise.

This activity works best in groups of four to eight participants. You can work with a theme or question as a starting point to help participants narrow down options and make proposals more concrete—for example, creating objects that have a specific function for the body.

1. Gather around the table. Each participant starts assembling a structure for the body using the materials laid on the table within timed five-minute sessions.

2. When five minutes are over, pass the structure to the person on your right.

3. You then receive a structure from the person on your left that you can add or take elements from. When five minutes are over again, pass the object on to your right.

4. Continue this process until everyone in the group has made an edit to each object and the objects have completed a full circle around the table.

5. Place all the 'final' objects on the table. Each person locates the object they originally started with, presents it on their body, and describes it. These descriptions can be function-oriented or abstract/poetic interpretations of their intention.

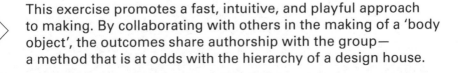

This exercise promotes a fast, intuitive, and playful approach to making. By collaborating with others in the making of a 'body object', the outcomes share authorship with the group— a method that is at odds with the hierarchy of a design house.

fashion for community

1. For the next event or gathering you may have (birthday party, baby shower, promotion party, etc.), find a group of individuals also attending that you have something in common with. They can be members of your immediate family, co-workers from the same department, classmates, or friends.

2. Find a fabric that can be shared with everyone in the group.

3. Ask your guests or members of the select group to include the fabric in their outfit for the event. This might mean creating a new piece, styling a headdress, draping it as a sash, wearing it as a scarf, etc.

4. Attend the event together. Do the items fashioned and worn have any significant effect on members of your group, the individual celebrating, or other guests at the event? What types of reactions do they elicit? How have members of your group shown their sense of individuality despite all of them wearing the same fabric?

5. Celebrate the creativity in your group by taking a group photo.

In some African cultures, fashion or the garments we wear are often markers of community and symbols of belonging. For example, when attending a wedding or a celebration such as a birthday, the hosts will usually ask guests or family members to wear a pre-selected fabric or headgear (*gele* for women and cap for men). The host or celebrant will select a particular fabric, order it in mass quantity, and distribute to family members or prospective guests to allow them to make or sew their own individually selected styles with the fabric.

In the Yoruba language, spoken across West Africa, this method of using matching fabrics for groups is known as *aso ebi* (family garments). *Aso* (or *asho*) translates to 'cloth' and *ebi* means 'family'. This term, *aso ebi*, is almost now universally used throughout Nigeria to identify this collective mode of dress, which is significant given that the country has over 250 ethnic groups, each fiercely asserting its cultural identity. In this way, garments in many African communities, in as much as they are an expression of your individual sense of identity and style, are primarily a marker of the community or the group to which you belong.

garments as correspon-dence

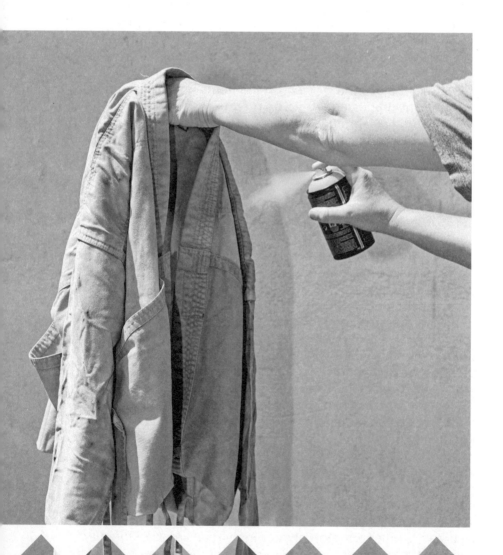

Choose a garment that you feel comfortable in and in which you have physical memories from your wardrobe (or the wardrobe of your partner or a friend).

Collect some debris from previous projects, such as textiles, paint, yarns, or fabric scraps.

Make a selection and apply these to your garment.

Choose a maker from your community of friends or allies. Invite them to respond to your garment by transforming it with tools and materials they love to work with in their practice.

Once your collaborator has returned the garment to you, start wearing it on a regular basis.

Reflect on how the garment has started a conversation between your practices and creative approaches; reflect on how this can inform your practice and support future collaborations.

When you feel ready, invite another inspiring maker to respond to your garment and give it another layer.

Document the different aspects of each collaboration: photo, piece, maker/partners, place, time, and techniques.

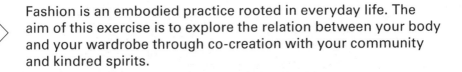

Fashion is an embodied practice rooted in everyday life. The aim of this exercise is to explore the relation between your body and your wardrobe through co-creation with your community and kindred spirits.

wearable to-getherness

Look at your calendar and pick a date. Make a list of friends and family members you would like to invite. Invite your guests to your home or any place that is both convenient and comfortable—this can be outside under a tree.

Here is an example of an invitation (you can send it in a printed, written, or verbal form):

'Let's make some garments together. I will prepare some tea and matcha biscuits for us. Do not worry if you can't sew or have not done this before; it will be fun. Please bring any materials you like, such as needles, yarn, fabrics, old T-shirts, thread, and buttons.
I look forward to seeing you on ___.'

Go through your fabrics at home and include all that you think could be used to create a garment; it is an excellent chance to include an heirloom such as a button you got from your grandma or a beloved old T-shirt.

1. Prepare the tea and food. Welcome your guests to the location you have chosen. Lay down all the materials you have and all the materials they brought. Consider forming a circle with the materials and sit around it.

2. Look at the materials together, tell their stories, and exchange ideas for how they might be used. You might like to draw some ideas out. Identify everyone's skills, curiosity, and comfort zone.

3. Get making. Try things you have never done before, such as sewing sleeves or embroidery.

4. Wear the piece(s) you made. It does not matter if the proportions are off or if the button does not fit the hole perfectly.

Laundry and dialogue

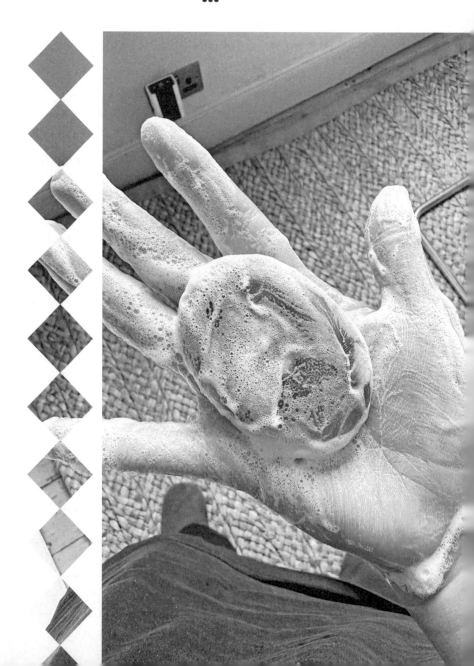

Much like the idobata kaigi of old times, this exercise invites you to reminisce about memories and thoughts about the garments you no longer wear by sharing experiences with other participants and washing your garments by hand. By creating a new experience and dialogue in relation to the memories of these garments, these forgotten garments will have a new value.

Gather a group of people, friends, strangers, or colleagues. Take one garment from your closet that you no longer wear but that you used to wear.

Put some cold or lukewarm water into the receptacle (get a receptacle such as a small pool that will have enough space for all the participant's garments).

Have everyone stand around the pool and wash their garments.

As you wash your garments, take turns (clockwise) telling stories about the garment that you no longer wear. During each turn, have all participants ask questions.

Once you are done speaking and answering questions, the next person starts talking about their garment.

Once everyone has finished speaking, wring out the garments and hang everyone's garments on a line to dry.

In Japan, there is a term called *idobata kaigi* [wellside meetings]. Before plumbing and washing machines proliferated, neighbours would gather around the shared well and chat and gossip while they did their laundry. Nowadays, because people wash their laundry at home, doing laundry is also an activity that doesn't invite communication.

portal

PORTAL is a participatory experience that provides a way to find the connections between garments and people. It encourages you to ask: How are different garments worn by different people related? In what ways are emotional and monetary values of garments connected? To whom does a garment actually belong?

Work in groups of three or more.

You will need:
- A large (several metres squared) piece of paper or or a large piece of white textile (i.e. a large bed sheet that you no longer use).
- Clear tape and coloured tape.
- Pens/markers.
- Garments (or footwear)—some garments from your wardrobe, a second-hand store, a friend.

Prepare your sheet of paper or fabric. This should be large enough to fit the outline of many garments (one per participant). You may need to stick together smaller pieces of paper to create a large sheet.

Place your garments on the sheet and draw a line around each with the coloured tape, leaving only the silhouette on the white surface.

Remove the garment (you should now see the shape of the garment as a kind of print). Draw any details of the garment on the white surface with a pen or pieces of tape; for example a zipper, pocket, or buttons.

On the sheet of paper next to each garment, answer the following questions:

1. What is it?
2. What is the material?
3. What is the colour?
4. What is the brand?
5. Where is it made?
6. In which year did you buy/receive it?
7. Was it a gift? (Yes/No).
8. Is it new or second-hand?
9. How much did it cost?
10. Did you buy it online or offline?
11. How often do you wear it? (Daily/weekly/monthly/yearly?)
12. How do you take care of it?
13. Is there a memory attached to it? If so, describe the memory.
14. Who made it?
15. How much would you pay for it today? (Less/same/more).
16. Is it yours?
17. How do you feel when you wear it?
18. Why did you put it on today?
19. What could be an alternative use for it?
20. What is its condition? Is there any visible damage?
21. What is its original function? (For example, Adidas Spezial sneakers are originally made for handball).

To find connections and relations within the group, connect the garments that share the same answers with the same coloured tape (i.e. red line could mean 'bought online', green line could mean the garment was a gift, purple line could refer to all cotton items). You will end up with a large canvas of shapes and criss-crossing lines across its surface, visually mapping and tracing the personal, economic, social, cultural, and political interconnections of your garment choices.

When you are done, you can fold the large paper sheet, cut open the fold lines where the tape is located to make a booklet, or even turn it into a work of art.

and
writing

Text in fashion—from the fashion caption to the show review—has been essential to the seasonal systems of production. Yet, as a profession, fashion writing has long been seen as a frivolous or lightweight undertaking, not worthy of the status of 'serious' journalism. The last ten years, however, has seen the emergence of critical fashion journals—such as *Vestoj*, *Viscose*, *Dune* and *Press & Fold*—and with them new practices of fashion criticism. This is represented in our book with methods for writing about fashion in expanded ways, from poetry to criticism, by Dinu Bodiciu, Nakako Hayashi, Anja Aronowsky Cronberg, and Dal Chodha.

Text can also be used as a tool to rethink, critique, and rewrite its commercial forces. Activities in this theme of 'Reading and Writing' mess up and experiment with fashion text. Shanzhai Lyric's '(Mis)translation Workshop' explores 'translation' as a tool for poetic writing and exploring the ubiquitous text in cultures of garments. Femke de Vries' 'Dictionary Dressing' and Gabriele Monti's

'Arbitrary Dictionary' use the form of the dictionary as a framework for looking at fashion as represented (or mis-represented) in the form of language, and thus how it affects our relationship to garments.

There are also exercises in this theme that use the artistic, poetic, and experimental dimensions of fashion text as the starting point to make or embellish garments. By working with text (instead, perhaps, of image), these exercises interrogate and question fashion's presumed materialities. For instance, exercises by Lou Hubbard and Liam Revell start with words to make garments.

ten questions and a poem

I keep six honest serving-men
(They taught me all I knew);
Their names are What and Why and When
And How and Where and Who. – Rudyard Kipling, 1902[1]

1. Who are you talking to?

2. Why do you want to join the system?

3. What is an artist?

4. Who decides what's original?

5. When is a work in progress finished?

6. Who says this is better than that?

7. How do you collapse a boundary without destroying the canon?

8. How do you reside in the in-between?

9. Where is this going?

10. When a rule doesn't break, how can it bend?

Vestoj is a space for thinking critically about fashion, a space for asking why we wear what we wear. Our work is guided by a manifesto that establishes our editorial ethics and practices, and we return to it in the making of each project. Below are questions that act as prompts to help you develop your own guiding manifesto for practice.

1　Rudyard Kipling, *Just So Stories* (London: AbeBooks, 1902).

"you wouldn't have noticed if you hadn't been told"

It is important that writers—especially those focused on fashion—observe rather than just look. When you are writing about fashion, such as reporting on a show, collection, or meeting with a designer, we need to understand 'how' you are seeing these experiences.

It is good practice to write down everything that you see. Not a diary, just a list.

Here are some examples of people who have done just that:

In prose: Zadie Smith's *A Hovering Young Man, Intimations* (2020).

In poem: C.P. Nield's 'Compost' (2020).

In essay: Georges Perec's 'Notes Concerning the Objects that are on my Work-table' (1976).

In hybrid text: my *SHOW NOTES* (2020)—my attempt at rearranging the messy notes I had pressed into my iPhone at fashion shows over a four-year period.

It is good practice to make the reader think—don't fear abstraction. They can handle it.

Now it is your turn. Write one hundred words about what is on your desk. If you are not sitting at a desk, then write about what is around you. What are you sitting on? What light source is above or beside you? Is the charger of your laptop getting hot? Is there a candle flickering violently? Are there half-chewed pens, fresh buttered crumbs, or tufts of cat hair? Write evocatively about the things you can see like Zadie Smith, C.P. Nield, Georges Perec, and I have done in the examples above. Be conscious that anything you are writing in this context is going to reveal more about you than you think. A friendly warning: 'a red pen' isn't just 'a red pen'. What kind of red is it? Is it 'a long red pen' or 'a red pen that is short'? Is it 'a thick red pen' or 'a thin red pen'?

You now have twenty minutes to write about the objects on your desk and around you.

You are exploring the importance of observational writing. The artist Martine Syms writes:

'Until recently I didn't think I had a studio practice. Last year I rented a large space with some friends and ended up writing a lot. My studio mate who was a painter would often ask me what I was working on. He told some mutual friends I was always on the computer.' — excerpt from "420" (2020) published in *STRAIT* (2021).

Now, open up Google. In the image search bar, type: 'karl lagerfeld choupette annie leibovitz desk'. Spend ten minutes looking at the photo that comes up. Write a description of this image.

conversation garments

A garment becomes a catalyst for a conversation.
The conversation becomes an embellishment on the
garment. The garment becomes a record of the encounter.
The encounter becomes the beginning of a design.

Arrange to meet up with somebody you know, or somebody you don't know.

Choose a garment, between the two of you, which can be written on. Something woven rather than knitted, with a flat, even surface, works best.

Decide on the type of discussion you want to have. It can be anything—getting to know each other personally, learning about each other's work practices, sharing stories, or a political debate.

Choose your writing tools. This can be fabric markers or a basic ballpoint pen, as long as it's easy to write with and to see on the fabric. You might want to use alternating colours, if you want to make the difference of your voices more apparent.

Set a time limit for the session, or agree on a point for it to end; for example, once there is no more space left on the garment. If you want the dialogue to unfold over a longer period, leave the garment in a space you can both access it for a chosen duration. You could also add dates in the text.

Meet. The only rule is: no speaking. You must converse entirely through written word, on the garment.

Place the garment flat on the floor or on a table. Begin the conversation, each writing your parts chronologically. Try to use all the surface areas—sleeves, collar, pockets, etc.

It might feel difficult at first to carry out a conversation 'naturally' in this way, but once you get started, it should start to flow and even become fun. If not, embrace the challenge.

Document the garment once it is ready, both on and off your bodies. Now you have a dialogue embedded in a garment.

Afterwards, you can further embellish the text, or some parts of it (for example, with embroidery); deconstruct the garment and use parts of the conversation as material for something new; or transcribe the text digitally for further applications.

Long-term interview

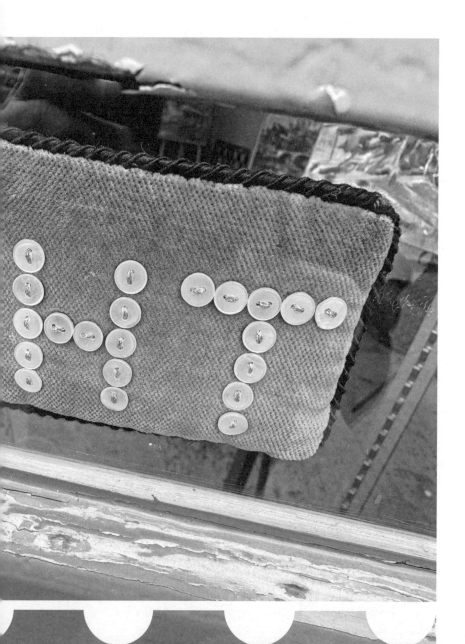

1. Plan an interview in a conversational style for a long period of time; one year, five years, ten years, or longer.

2. Record your long-term conversation in a notebook.

3. Start by talking about something casual. Try to continue the conversation from time to time.

4. After each conversation, reflect on what you did not understand and prepare new questions for next time.

5. When you sense points of change in your subject, embrace them carefully and wait for them to unfold in conversation.

Spend time with your interviewee doing things together, allowing the conversation to be non-hierarchical, full of surprises and discoveries, and lead to mutual exchanges. For example, you might share your interests related to beauty in daily life, such as films, books, or flowers. Or you might do something together or in parallel. For example, raise the same bulbs throughout winter, read the same book, or watch the same film. Exchange the process or results when it is done.

Fashion media tends to focus on immediacy and speed. This exercise attempts to slow down the writing process with a long-term interview. Everyday conversation can lead to an interview book or an exhibition. The key is to choose an interviewee based on your personal interest and make the conversation non-hierarchical so that it can last for a long time period. Share your interests and do things together, such as reading books or watching films or growing the same flower.

wearing our- selves on our T-shirts

Think about your own lived experience and of the ways that you think you differ from fashion ideals or norms in the media. This might be in relation to gender, race, size, or any other facet you can identify. Come up with some words or a symbol that represents your 'difference'. You could be oblique or overt in how you represent this; it could be, for example, a meal, a colour, a cliche, a description, a definition, a subcultural phenomenon, or slang. This reflective process might include collecting materials including objects and paraphernalia.

Using tape, create a graphic on a T-shirt (maybe one from your wardrobe or a second-hand store) that represents (and celebrates) the differences you have identified. This can be crudely constructed with letters, text, or symbols. If you don't have tape just cut out letters/words/shapes from paper (or any other collected material) and lay it on top of your T-shirt.

This exercise can be done in a group or individually. At the close of the exercise, come together to share your creations and, more importantly, consider the multiple ways that people may be marginal to fashion's ideals. Take time to see and hear what others have to say through their stories. Consider how fashion might be more inclusive and how you might practise empathy through a design practice of allyship.

The T-shirt has a storied history as a communicator of social resistance and activism. This activity encourages the consideration of marginal identities in fashion by reflecting on our own lived experience. It proposes a starting point to learn about the marginalization of others through the medium of the ubiquitous T-shirt.

floating signifiers

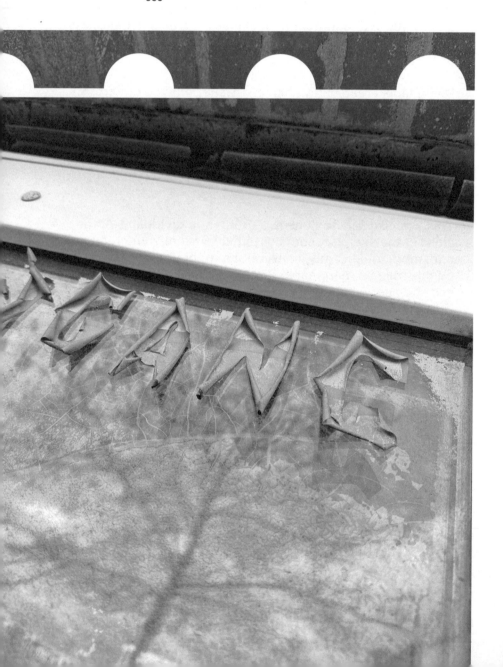

1. Notice the text on other people's garments (in the street, your workplace, or a public library). Take notes and pictures (if possible). Make small drawings next to the text to remember the typography, the colours, font sizes, and positions of the text on these garments.

2. Once you have collected around fifteen examples, take a sheet of paper and start organizing them. Look for patterns. For example, how many have a sporty font? How often do you find references to American high schools? How many attempt to be inspirational or motivational?

3. Start drawing lines between examples or clusters of examples. Undo the order. Make the signifiers float!

4. Distil a group of four strong outcomes that are a mix of words, typography, colour, and references (to sports or American high schools, for example). Print one (or more) of these on a shirt and wear it.

'Floating signifiers' is an exercise that uses text found on garments and makes it as weird, nonsensical, and 'floating' as possible. Words that appear on garments are affected by placement, typography, and colour—as such, their meaning is warped. This method de-signifies text found on garments (empties it of meaning) and then re-signifies it (gives it a new meaning through collage, typography, and mixing of words and positions).

[mis]trans- lation workshop

A T-shirt (or tee shirt, or tee) is a style of unisex fabric shirt, nameb after the T shape of the body and sieeves. It is normal-ly associated with short sleeves, a round neck line known as a crew neck, with no collar.

Translating poetry is a tricky task. Shanzhai lyrics, the non-standard text found on garments often made in China but worn around the world, are especially slippery. With their hybridity, irregular grammar, spelling, and punctuation—often including strings of apparent gibberish—shanzhai lyrics resist translation. Drawing from a pile of archival poetry-garments, this exercise invites you to respond to this challenge, creatively translating shanzhai language. Follow your intuitions and impulses. Have fun with the (im)possibility of smooth translation. How can the act of translation be a mode of appreciating the ecstatic, experimental language of shanzhai garments and the values they put forth?

Some Things to Consider
- How can a translation embrace difference, unintelligibility, complexity, absurdity, and playfulness through nonstandard grammar, spelling, and punctuation?
- How can we translate text into hybrid tongues that make space for the questions, reflections, and insights that emerge between languages?
- How might a collective translation process reflect the ways shanzhai processes re-envision notions of authorship, ownership, and originality?

Some Things to Try
- Translate into an image (graphic translation): consider the words as images and redraw the poem in another alphabet or writing system by choosing letters or characters that most closely resemble the shapes of the original.
- Translate into sound (homophonic translation): ask someone to read the poem aloud to you and compose a new poem by choosing words in a different language that most closely resemble the sounds of the original.
- Translate using a dictionary (lexical translation): translate word for word using a dictionary. Approximate as closely as possible for clusters of letters that do not form recognizable words.

dictionary pressings

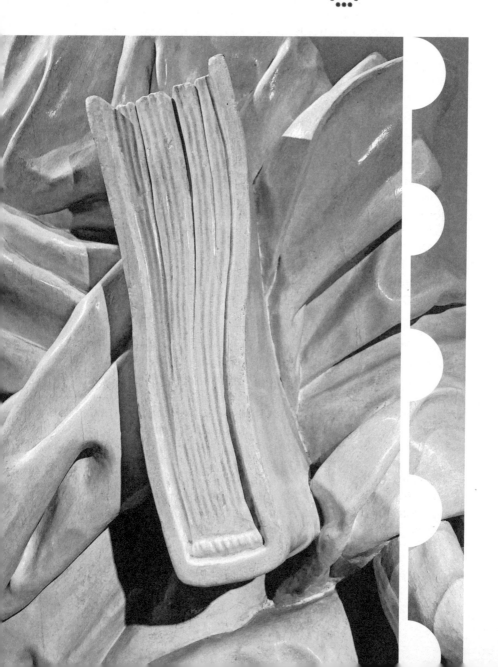

Pick a garment, maybe one that you are wearing.

Note down what it looks like: its style, what it is called, what it means, and what you associate with it.

Now look up the garment's definition in a dictionary (online or in a book).

Use the definition as a basis for designing a new garment. Stay true to the contents of the definition: use it as a set of instructions for your form. What is present in the description and what is not? (For example, does the material matter and which body part does it cover? Does a sweater have to have two sleeves and one hole for the neck, or can it also be the other way around? Can it be multiplied?).

Use any kind of 'material' you like: you can draw, make, or write this garment.

Reflect on the differences to this new form as it relates to the original definition.

Garments are loaded with symbols and references ingrained by culture and the fashion industry. They are objects dense with style, meaning, and value. This meaning thus determines the way we look at garments and 'design' fashion, leading to a self-referential (style and value) system. This exercise explores this system of meaning by reducing a garment to its dictionary description. A definition undressed of style, culture, or fashion. It places everyone into a fashion-amateur position and offers new ways of understanding garments and fashion.

arbitrary
pictionary

This exercise works best in groups of three to four people.

Each group identifies a limited number of keywords that group members feel relate to the fashion system and its practices.

For each word, the group collectively writes a definition and creates an accompanying visual based on the research and creative interests of each group member.

Compile these definitions together in a new collective 'dictionary'.

The dictionary is a useful format for defining and identifying fashion. It is an object that is also arbitrary, in motion, 'wrong'. In this exercise, the dictionary is used to generate visual form to describe and interpret design processes—both material and immaterial.

Note: This exercise was developed in a course at
      IUAV University of Venice. Each academic year
      students self-publish an *Arbitrary Dictionary*.

writing a garment

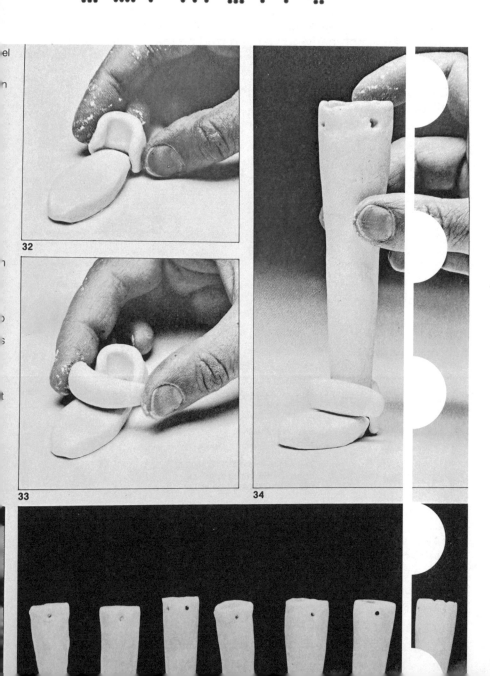

32

33

34

1. Work with a friend or colleague.

2. Choose a garment you own, a garment designed by someone else, or simply imagine a garment.

3. Describe the garment in writing. Focus on incorporating the mood of the item or generating an atmosphere rather than trying to be explicit in terms of construction or materials. Allow space for interpretation. For example, try to avoid the following type of description: 'shirt in white cotton poplin with French seams, fused collar and cuffs, and eight white buttons on the centre front placket'. Instead, be imaginative and illustrate with words elements such as the disposition, tenor, or character of the garment.

4. When you have finished writing, exchange your text with your partner.

5. Working independently (keeping your work secret from each other until the end), make a sketch of the garment you wrote about; keep this sketch for yourself, as a reference.

6. Now read your partner's text and sketch it in full colour. Draft a sewing pattern of the sketch, make a toile, and select a fabric.

7. Gift the garment to your partner.

8. Compare the imagined garment (the sketch each of you kept secret) with the real one (that each of you have made).

When fashion items are presented/described in written format, we visualize them differently. 'Writing a Garment' explores the role of interpretation and subjectivity in fashion as it is described.

Head butt toe

Whatever you do, wherever you are, make do and be thrifty.
Make over, overdo, oversee, misstep. Just be sure to do it,
go head-over-heels. Find your means. Don't be mean. What
do you mean?

1. Work in groups. In five minutes, on paper, list on separate lines as many types of apparel as you can name.

2. Read to the group your list and eliminate any repeated words.

3. Tear each word as a single strip of paper and place into a hat.

4. Have each participant draw out three strips of paper.

5. Combine each word to make six sets. For example, the selected words 'cap', 'socks' and 'bra', when coupled, become:
    cap bra
    cap socks
    socks cap
    socks bra
    bra cap
    bra socks

6. Use the second word of each apparel combination to determine the function of the new apparel you are to make from the object named by the first word:
    a bra is made from caps
    socks are made from caps
    caps become socks
    bras become socks
    a cap is made from a bra
    socks are made from a bra or two

7. Thrift shop—or raid your someone's wardrobe—for your designated apparel. You may need a few of each item.

8. Perform as though on a catwalk, and record on camera your new apparel: on the body, off the body, discarded.

9. Name your collection. Publish or bust!

This group exercise aims to disinhibit, dislocate, and review the clad body. It uses language to disrupt and re-imagine garments' conventional function of being right, appropriate, or fitting. Strategies of restraint, thrift, and making do promote ingenuity, craft, and unconditional outcomes.

Lexical Fashion Design

Explore an environment (it can be physical or digital). As you do, write down, draw, or photograph (or a mix of all three) words you encounter. Don't overthink it, but choose words whose appearance, sound, or personal associations appeal to you (choose eighty to one hundred words; a surplus of words is beneficial). If you like, invent neologisms from the words collected.

Use the words to compose a poem. Think of an aesthetic you want to achieve with their arrangement. Remember, poetry is a form of making. Play with the syntax, parataxis, and rhythm of the poem. When composing the poem, consider how fashion is represented: its gestures, its postures, its bodies, its moods, its atmospheres, and the worlds it constructs.

Consider the poem as the medium for a suggestive inquiry. Disregard the words' denotative meaning. Make free associations. What do the words—individually or in 'sentences'—evoke or propose? How can you translate these ideas through fabrication and in materials? How will the aesthetic in material exploration respond to that of the poem?

Some further ideation activities you can do:
- Use words as verbs and apply them as actions to materials.
- Render words from the poem as colours, trims, surfaces, silhouettes, and textures.
- Develop associative definitions for words and explore these definitions in material form.
- When developing an aesthetic, don't think about resolved outcomes (such as garments and accessories). The fragments you produce are ideas pointing towards a design concept.

Fashion has a lexicon of words, and many of these words refer to physical objects. But fashion changes, and so the lexicon changes too. This lexical change imparts ambiguity to words and material. This exercise exploits the ambiguity of fashion words to search for an aesthetic that is unknown or undetermined.

Poetry as Translation

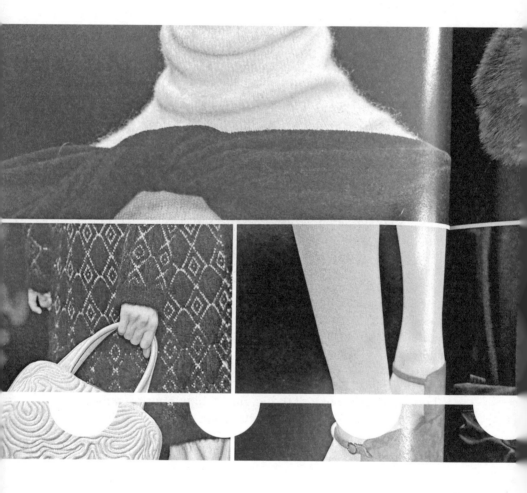

You will need: a book, magazine, or device for reading.
A long-form interview, essay, or article—perhaps one you
have been wanting to read for a while, but haven't been able
to commit the time or energy to.

Skim read the text, noticing key phrases, terminology, and shifts in tone. Extract words or lines to create a poem, adding new punctuation if necessary. The poem does not need to describe what's in the interview, it can be completely different.

Here is an example using an interview between Shonagh Marshall (writer, lecturer, and editor of the Denier newsletter) and Kimberly Jenkins (lecturer, researcher, and founder of the Fashion and Race Database).[1]

the course came into being, personally speaking
it was self-serving in a way
a laboratory of ideas
a therapeutic space
a one-woman show, robust, rich, immersive, but
racial tensions were high
I was thrust out onto the front lines
couldn't be any more conspicuous

the climate accelerated
touched, impacted, so rich
how do we start?
where do we begin?
moving through the centuries, colonization after colonization
a fashion utopia
wanting, wanting, wanting, and then throwing away

Inspiration for this exercise comes from Lindsay Jordan at University of the Arts London, who often uses such tasks to explore key themes in academic texts.

This exercise is a speculative and experimental research method for engaging with longer form texts and interviews. It employs poetic analysis, which can conceptualize and unlock creative themes in qualitative data, essentially re-organizing a text into something more free and expressive.

1   Shonagh Marshall, 'A Conversation with Kimberly Jenkins,' Fashion Denier, July 26, 2021. www.fashiondenier.com/conversations/a-conversation-with-kimberly-jenkins

Text as material

Choose a piece of text that relates to your practice (a topic or theme you are interested in). This can be a poem, journal article, page/chapter from a book, newspaper article—it should link in some way to what you do and what you find important in your work. If you're not sure where to start, you can choose a page or a chapter from a seminal text about fashion.

Print out or photocopy the text twice, single-sided. You may want to play with the size of the text by printing it out on different paper and font sizes. Lay these copies out on a table. Have a pencil or a highlighter, scissors or a knife and cutting mat, some blank sheets of paper, a glue stick, and tape ready to use.

Take the first copy of the text and before you read it, decide on a rule or pattern for selection (all verbs, all words that start with a capital letter, etc.). Underline or highlight the words that belong to this selection rule or pattern throughout the text. You should not read the text or try to understand it; you should just skim through looking for the specific words, warming up, and getting familiar with it as material.

Take the second copy of the text and as you slowly read through it, underline or highlight the words or sentences that speak to you. Do this intuitively. It might be sentences that you find striking, that you agree or disagree with, or phrases or single words that connect to your own ideas. Once finished, carefully cut out each sentence or group of words that you have underlined and set them aside. Try to cut out the text in a way that leaves the remaining page readable.

Now you have a collection of loose pieces of highlighted text. Start to arrange these into groups: you can try to make new sentences or simply create relationships/associations between words or sentences that were previously unrelated. Make three different versions of your groupings or categories. Photograph each one before starting afresh and making a new set. If you need ideas or more words at this stage, look back at the first copy in which you highlighted a 'pattern', as it might give you a new angle or way to read your collection. You can also cut out some of these words if they help you to make interesting new configurations.

Once you are happy with certain new sentences or groupings, start to arrange them on a blank page and stick them down. Leave space between different ideas/thoughts on the page, or use separate pages if you prefer.

Once you have completed your word assemblage, read your new text out loud to someone and have a conversation about it.

When we read text, especially theory, it can be difficult to find a 'way in' to understand its content and how it can be applied to creative practice and daily life. Using text as a material, this exercise can begin to dissolve anxieties around text/writing and open up playful possibilities for the production and appropriation of meaning.

making,
tracing

Behind contemporary industrial fashion and its promise for a sustainable future looms a modernist industrial system of production based on capitalist values of growth, distributed labour, profits at any cost. Exercises under the theme of 'Making, Finding, Tracing' reimagine how fashion is produced and what it produces. This includes methods for the fashion process: construction methods, form-making, technical innovation, and material explorations. In the place of Western European flat pattern-making, draping, and fitting the rigid dress form are alternative actions such as making, finding, tracing, sorting, randomizing, and more.

In the university classroom, traditional pattern-making and construction techniques are being rewritten. This shift is represented by exercises that rethink construction conventions and the confining boundaries of the patternmaking block. We see this in Andrea Eckersley's 'Abstract Form-making', Ashish Dhaka and Sonika Soni Khar's 'The Circle as Garment Form', and Dinu Bodiciu's 'Shadowear', which uses the wearer's shadow as the basis for design, and Lidya Chrisfens' 'Blind Draping'. Whilst these look at 'form' in the construction of garments, other exercises in this theme present methods for material exploration in fashion. Stéphanie Baechler and Francesca Capone look at the infrastructure of our garments—woven cloth—exploring its construction and connecting it with cultural histories and their threads. Several exercises in this theme also embrace systems of chance as a way to defer, even forgo, the onus of control altogether. We are invited to give the design process over to the throw of the dice in Anne Karine Thorbjørnsen's contribution.

The Dice Game

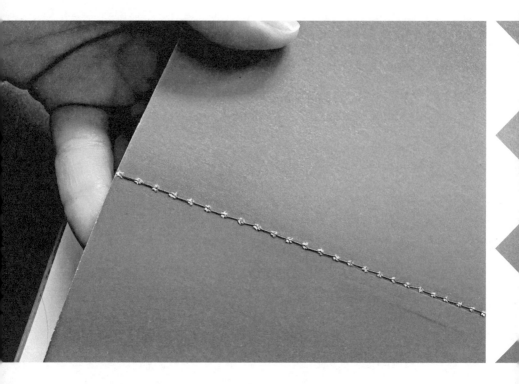

The following instructions use form-making on a mannequin, but you can adapt this method for any stage of the creative process.

This exercise uses a die.

Lay out a selection of materials and research you are working with. You can choose tools that you feel comfortable working with, that are unfamiliar, or from other disciplines. Selecting your tools is where your control ends.

Decide how many actions you will include in this exercise (one to six) by throwing the die.

Here are some ideas for actions (but you could write your own):
1. Construct on a mannequin.
2. Work on the floor.
3. Destroy.
4. Make it look 'pretty'.
5. Work blindfolded.
6. Work one handed.

- Decide (by throwing the die) how many minutes you have to complete the exercise (one to six).
- Decide (by throwing the die) how many materials you will use (one to six).
- Decide (by throwing the die) how many techniques you will employ (one to six).
- Decide (by throwing the die) which techniques you will use.

Here are some ideas of techniques (but you could write your own):
1. Handstitch.
2. Tape.
3. Knot.
4. Pins.
5. Strips.
6. Throw.

Document the process with images and drawings.

Be true to the exercise and do not cheat, even if you feel discomfort and don't want to do what the die tells you. Acknowledging the negative feelings as well as the positive ones is part of the process. Be curious about the ugliness and chaos that might occur, as well as the beauty. What we find ugly tends only to be what we are not used to—and this could be where you discover something new.

This exercise uses dice as decisive tools in the design process. It can be used in every part of the development process of making; from developing visual research material, design development, to construction. Dice can be tools to explore creative possibilities as well as unburden you from existing aesthetic boundaries.

abstract
form making

1. Find a small 3D object that you can fit onto your hand.

2. Make a paper pattern for this object and construct it in fabric.

3. Scale the pattern up to the dimensions of a body and construct it in fabric.

4. Cut one hole into the large scale fabric object and place it on the body.

5. Cut three more holes to allow for head and limbs.

6. Turn the large scale fabric object upside down, sideways, or any which way and put arms or legs or one arm and one leg through the holes.

7. Draw and photograph at least six different ways the fabric object can be worn on the body.

8. Take six designs for bodies dressed with fabric objects and refine into garments.

Using alternative garment shapes that challenge traditional fashion silhouettes and cuts, this exercise asks participants to experiment with rendering random objects in fabric at different scales to dress a body and explore new potential in fashioning the figure.

Note: This exercise was conceived as part of the Bachelor of Fashion (Design) (Honours) curriculum in the School of Fashion and Textiles at RMIT University, Melbourne

abstract pattern-making

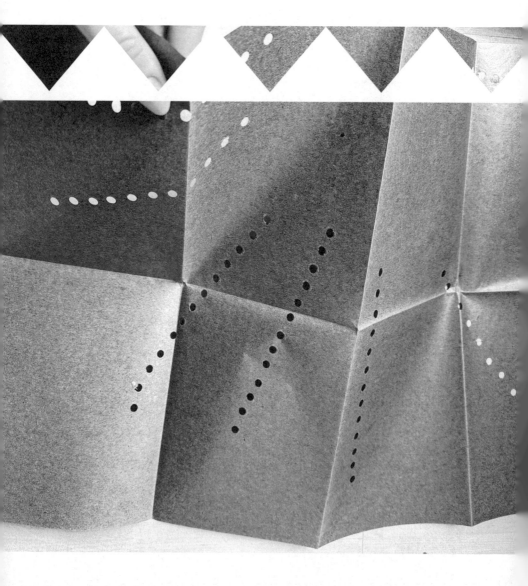

1. Find a piece of paper of any size, preferably of rectangular shape.

2. Fold it in any way you want; you can follow it into a simple shape or fold it randomly.

3. Unfold the paper and trace the folded lines.

4. Number every section, document with a photo, then cut along the folded lines.

5. Rearrange all the pieces of paper into a 3D shape. You can make extra cuts if needed.

6. Once you have the 3D shape, document with photos. Before taking the pieces apart, take notes of the order in which you put the pieces together so that you can put them back together again.

7. You now have a pattern that you can use. Try assembling the pattern at large-scale (by scaling it up) or small-scale.

8. Apply it to the body in different ways and document with photos and notes as you experiment.

The way in which patternmaking shapes the body into a 2D map (by indicating coordinates, lines, and measurements) can be very rigid and wasteful of materials. This activity challenges traditional patternmaking techniques and ways of shaping the body.

shadowear

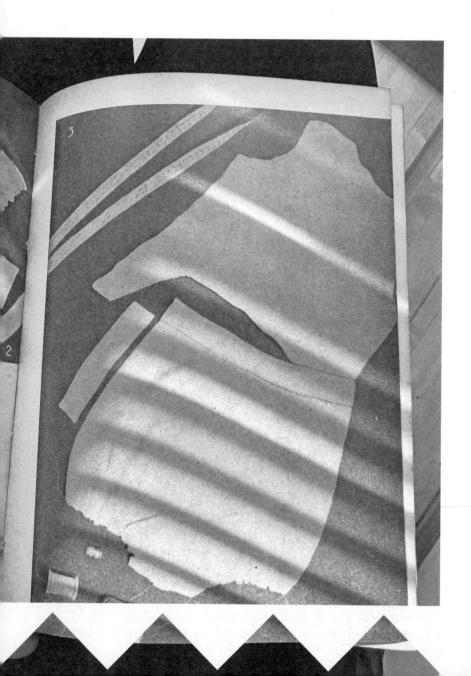

1. Using a natural (the sun or the moon) or artificial light source, project a shadow of yourself onto a blank wall or surface. Play with your body's shadow and take a few photos of some interesting shapes that you produce.

2. Print the shadow image onto an A4 piece of paper.

3. With a coloured pen, trace the outlines and seam lines of the garments that you were wearing. Observe the posture of the shadow to imagine where seams and all garment details could have been. The outcome can be very distorted.

4. Scale your A4 sketch up to life size. Then turn your Shadowear form into pattern pieces. Cut and sew. Try the garment and enjoy how it drapes in reality.

Shadowear is an exercise that shifts attention from the 3D body to the 2D projected shadow by imagining 3D projections as the basis for a garment's construction. It is an iterative design approach that flattens the body and removes gender and cultural signifiers.

the circle as garment form

Creating patterns for a garment involves an intimate interaction between the body, the outer form, and the space between the body and form. Consciously or unconsciously, this interaction is fundamental to the development of all garments. This exercise explores the radial geometry, bias, and drape of the circle. The circle can be plucked, cinched, layered, constructed, or deconstructed to create forms.

1. Measure a region of the body (upper torso, shoulder, and arms) to identify the radius/diameter of your first circle.

2. Cut at least two circles so that the body can be sandwiched between them.

3. The circumference of the circle can be stitched or pinned leaving strategic openings for the neckline, limbs, waist, and hem.

    Further explorations can be done using any combination of the following actions:

    Add or subtract a circle, or a fragment of a circle, onto another circle.

    Shift the centre of the circle to explore its behaviour and drape. Explore this action in different fabrics (woven, knit, felt, etc.).

    Add a circle to a basic pattern piece on strategic points to accentuate or warp fit.

deletion
pressing

This exercise applies the action of redacting to self-styling. By adding black rectangles of fabric to an existing outfit, the wearer is able to obfuscate unwanted visual details and to produce their own new look. This approach activates wearing as an accessible mode of making and explores how redaction can be reframed as a productive act. In doing so, 'Deletion Dressing' invites wearers to reimagine existing garments and mass-produced garments by editing them to fashion a unique self-image.

1. Make the redactions. Create a series of rectangles in black fabric (these can be made using any material of any dimension). Try to make a variety of sizes and to use the entire piece of fabric. Attach several one-metre long ties to each piece. The ties can be attached anywhere.

2. Take your redactions and find a space with a mirror where you feel comfortable dressing. For example, the room where you usually get dressed.

3. Apply your redactions to the outfit you are wearing. The redactions can be strapped, tied, or draped over your garments.

4. Observe how each redaction simultaneously removes visual details and adds them, altering both how you appear to yourself and how you will be perceived by others. Consider how you can strategically apply the redactions to make your outfit more closely reflect how you would like to be seen.

5. Apply more redactions, observing what is removed and what is added as you go. You may document the process with sketches, photos, or video.

6. Once you have applied all the redactions and feel that your new 'look' is complete, wear it out somewhere: to the shop to buy milk, to your friend's engagement party, to mow your lawn, or to the office.

blind draping

1. Prepare a body or mannequin form and pins. Also prepare your material palette. This can include: trims, a few different textures and weights of material, lengths of fabric, jewellery, garments, etc.

2. Close your eyes. Calm your mind for a minute to free yourself from any surrounding disturbance. Think of a memory or scenario.

3. Touch everything in your material palette, then start to drape the fabric on the body or form. Let your thoughts lead your hand.

4. Continue draping until you are ready to stop.

5. When you are done, open your eyes and bring your awareness to the present.

6. Examine the drape piece; write down your thoughts and make sketches of what you have created. The draped result could be the basis for design development or a final piece of its own.

This exercise invites you to close your eyes while draping. By removing the visual aspects, this will allow you to focus on the materiality, texture, balance, weight, movement, and feeling of the garment.

Designing with the body

You will need:
- A 3D laser scanner (in-phone app or any device).
- Tinfoil.
- Bubble wrap.
- Different textures and transparencies of fabric from varying colours or plastic bags.
- Collected leaves/twigs/plants.
- Any other scrap material with interesting form or texture.

1. Select any choice or combination of collected materials and start wrapping and building these around your body. Try not to start with a pre-determined or stylized shape; instead, be intuitive and experimental.

2. Ask a friend to scan your body with a 3D scanning app or tool.

3. Explore the result and continue developing experiments, either by changing materials or adding new materials over the top of your silhouette.

4. Reflect on the generated experiments and explore how they can become a study of forms emerging from your bodily movements and interaction with materials when captured by the scanner. What unexpected shapes do these scans reveal? Can you use these scans to inform your garment design process? How do these experiments generate a different perception of the body outside pre-established parameters and aesthetics? What does it mean to see yourself as a mutable and fluid entity in contrast with the 'sealed', static figure of the mannequin? How might this awareness influence the way you design?

Traditionally, fashion design begins with the mannequin as the site of garment production. The mannequin is an idealized figure of perfection and a generic blueprint to standardize bodies. This activity replaces the mannequin with your own body as the starting point for design, and as a way to disrupt its reductive framework.

fade to clay

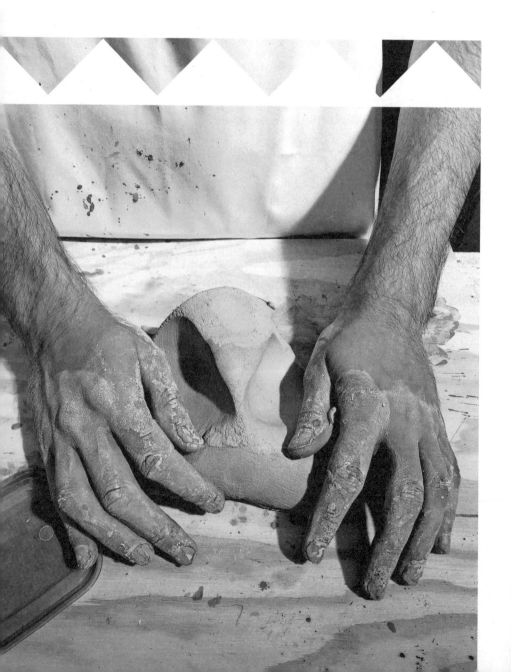

1. Work with a clay extruder—a tool that forces clay through a metal die to form coils. If you don't have an extruder, you can carefully roll out clay coils, as long as you can, by hand. Create seven to ten clay coils.

2. Form your coils into a weaving structure and pattern. For example, you could try to make a net structure.

3. Add colour. Colour some clay with pigment and extrude more lines to add to your structure. You can also use different coloured clay, such as black clay.

4. Cut some small coils and place them on top of your woven experiment.

5. Take a rolling pin and flatten the experiment.

6. Continue to experiment with the above steps with more clay coils and make different textile structures.

7. Draw, photograph, or scan at least six clay experiments. These become the basis for design development for the body or a speculative textile.

The aim of this exercise is to make alternative garment shapes or textile structures in clay that challenge traditional forms and materiality of fashion by experimenting with clay coils (using a clay extruder).

conceptualizing weaving

Consider your body and how it functions in relation to the loom. How do the warp, the weft, the shuttles, the heddles, and the treadles all interact with your body? What does this look like on a floor loom? What about an industrial loom?

Consider your identity in relation to the loom. What is your personal heritage? How does this heritage relate to textile creation? What is the history of these processes? Are they simple or complex? What potential do they have in the future?

Consider time and the time taken to weave in relation to the woven product; think of the woven product as a metaphor of time. Can you map the labour involved in the woven garments you are wearing?

Consider the place or environment you are working in—from macro (planet, country, state, city) to micro (the studio, sounds, and sensations of weaving). How does this place relate to what you are weaving?

Consider your materials. Where do they come from? Are they native to your environment? How do they reflect their geography? Are they ethically made and/or ecologically-sustainable?

Consider weaving as code, and the likeness of this code to digital coding (zeros and ones). Are there ways in which weaving and these interactions are connected? Where can you uncover weaving in the digital interfaces and experiences of daily life?

Consider how you might reinvent an existing technique. First identify the technique and then sketch out twenty ways to recreate it.

Consider the architecture of the loom. Is it possible to re-design or re-structure this? What kind of fabric would your new loom produce?

Solve a contemporary problem through weaving. Consider this on a large scale: social, domestic, maternity, communication, religion, science, medical, political, farming and food, transportation, travel, hospitality, and housing problems. Or consider this on a local scale: personal relationships, your own wardrobe, for your pets, at your job, in your domestic environment, etc.

A contemporary weaving practice represents a recognition and elevation of a form of textile creation that has had great significance throughout the history of human civilization. This exercise prompts reflection on the meaning and relevance of weaving and asks how to ground such a practice in social and technological history. The creation of cloth has long served the purposes of fashion and interiors but it has also served as a radical substrate for coded communication on the fringes of dominant society. Literacy did not become common until the mid-twentieth century, and those who had the skill to stitch may not have had the access or education to record their points of view in written word. Cloth served this population as a mode of communication for which to make their mark, and examples of this tradition exist on every continent. Creating contemporary work within the canon of cloth comes with this rich tradition of subversion. As such, it calls for new inquiries to be made into how weaving practices can build upon their own history.

re-viewin

images

Fashion objects are generally sold using imagery. Evocative images of fashion and the smooth, perfect objects they feature elicit individual desires and distance a consumer from the real conditions of production. The garments we wear are mystified as a result of the multiple industrial processes, from manufacturing to advertising. How can a consumer take responsibility for ethical design, while specific details of how garments are produced in the industrial fashion system are generally suppressed (or at the very least, styled) by fashion images and media?

Exercises in 'Re-viewing Images' examine the fashion image as the primary medium for communication in fashion. This is often where we, as consumers, first encounter a garment. This theme includes exercises that analyze and critique the 'fashion image' as a distinct phenomenon. Beata Wilczek's 'Fashion Image Questionnaire' audits the fashion image using a 'questionnaire as a tool for poetic, abstract, and situated knowledge production'.

The fashion image often bears distinct features—a model's pose, casting, lighting and framing—that generate desire. Exercises in this theme interrogate the smooth, high-production, digital facade of the contemporary fashion image via its key ingredients. For example, Chet Julius Bugter's 'Re-enacting the Fashion Image' places us in the body of the fashion image via the familiar trope of the fashion pose, producing a bootleg version by the participant. Saul Marcadent and Federico Antonini's 'Bootleg Magazine' also explores the radical act of 'bootlegging' by copying an entire fashion publication as a way to closely interrogate its form and content.

The image is also a fundamental element in the styling and creation of fashion editorial, which can lead to a system of self-perpetuation. Mary-Lou Berkulin's 'The Elusive vs. the Everyday' offers a method for breaking the mould of fashion image-making by making a communal mood board of found images. And Sanne Karssenberg's method, 'Wearers Past and Present' dives into a photograph as the starting point to research and write about garments and their social history, giving us a tool to rediscover things forgotten in the past.

re-enacting the fashion image

It is best to do this exercise by yourself.

First, get yourself a copy of a high-end, authoritative, luxury fashion magazine such as *Vogue*, *Elle*, or *Harper's Bazaar*.

Make sure you are dressed in such a way that you can move freely. Take off any accessories, glasses, and shoes.

Start browsing through the magazine. Check the advertisements, advertorials, editorials, and photoshoots. How do these images make you feel? Do you feel attracted or repulsed by them? Are you envious? Do they make you dream? Or do they make you feel neutral? Mark every image that you feel strongly about.

Next, set up and start a video recording. Make sure your full body is captured in the frame.

Now it is time to re-enact. Starting at the beginning of the magazine, work your way through the images you have marked. Look very closely at each photograph. Try to replicate exactly how the model's body has been positioned. Be aware of how your arms are angled, fingers are placed, and how your legs are stretched and crossed. If a model is wearing high-heeled shoes, make this position—standing on one toe—the last step in the re-enactment. Remember also to take the mirrored perspective of the photograph into account.

Hold the pose for as long as your body is able to.

Capture your reflection on each of the poses as specifically as possible and archive it together with the video (or video stills).

The aim of this exercise is to become aware of the influence of authoritative fashionable imagery on your body. By re-enacting and embodying poses found in the images of a fashion magazine, you are invited to question the representation of the body within the industrial fashion system.

bootleg
magazine

1. Get hold of a physical copy of an editorial object such as a magazine, a fanzine, a catalogue, a lookbook, or brochure. Analyze the visual and textual contents, the editorial style, the graphic design and typography, the paper stock, the circulation figure, the cover price (where suitable), and the distribution. This enables you to talk about the object, but also about the context and the processes that generated it.

2. Produce an altered, bootlegged, parasitic, evil-twin version of the chosen object through additions, margin notes, cuts, deletions, alterations, disassembly, removals, overlays, overprints, scans, and photocopies. Create your bootleg in assonance-dissonance with the original contents. In this phase, it is important to consider the objects for their three-dimensional value.

3 Consider how your interventions might be reproduced in a series: every action must face the conditions and constraints of editorial design, readership, commerce.

There are multiple ways to channel strong conceptual processes, overturning the original content, even using mundane production techniques. In the second step, it could be useful to work with a printer or a graphic designer to reflect on the difference between typography, copy shop, screen printing, and bookbinding. You are encouraged to consider performative approaches.

A fashion image is not just a question of fashion, but an abstract, undecipherable, and unformulated bond between things, people, their allures, and their desires. Starting from this thought, this exercise ignites reflection on the printed image of fashion as it appears on the page. It also proposes a way of reactivating fashion printed material and bringing it back to circulation.

Note: This exercise was developed within the context of the Publishing Atelier at IUAV University of Venice.

replica
relay race

1. Work in three to five groups of four.

2. Assign each member a number (from one to four).

3. Give participants in the first group an identical image of a luxury fashion item. Instruct them to copy this image through drawing or collage, using the reference image, and adding one modification. This step should be done individually, away from others, and in three minutes.

4. When participants in the first group are finished, have them deposit their modified images in a box that is not visible to the other groups.

5. Give participants in the second group the modified images made by participants in the first group that were deposited in the box, with the same instructions.

6. Continue the relay race until every group has made a modified image.

7. Collect all the images from the box; shuffle and then place them on the floor.

8. Arrange the images on a scale with 'replica' and 'original' on opposite ends.

    By allowing participants to visualize and contextualize the process of modification, this exercise presents an opportunity to highlight the complexities and subjectivities behind derivative fashion systems and provides a starting point for an in-depth discussion. How do we determine what is an original design, a modified object, or a replica? Is it be possible for a 'replica' to become an original design on its own terms? What are the grey areas between appropriation and appreciation? How can designers and consumers navigate such complexities and subjectivities fairly and ethically (for all parties)?

Conditions of value, appreciation, and appropriation are issues that are highly relevant in current fashion discourse. This exercise explores the complexities and subjectivities behind 'the original' and 'the replica'. Can a replica possibly become an original design?

ways of
seeing
(an object)

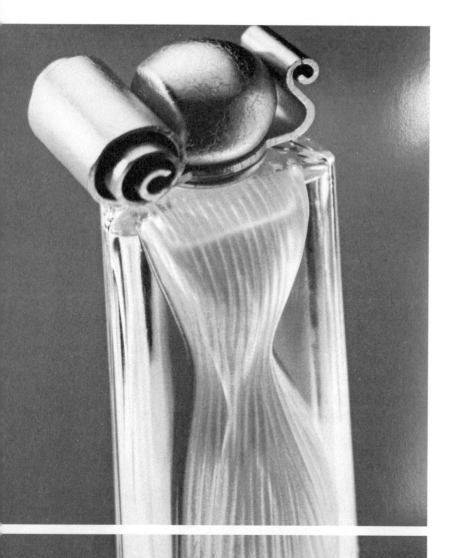

Select an object that you are working with or that you draw visual inspiration from (such as a garment or accessory).

Record your object as a specimen. Use the camera like a scientist would to record how it looks; do this as clearly and objectively as possible in a neutral setting (for example, against a white backdrop from its front, back, and sides).

Document your object in 'real space'. Use the camera as if you are a photojournalist documenting a 'real' chance encounter with the item as you might find it in an everyday setting.

Abstract your object. Photograph your item as if it were a texture/shape to be used in an artistic, abstract composition. Focus on interesting ways of depicting its colour, texture, and shape through exploring camera angles and cropping.

Narrate your object. Photograph your item as part of a demonstrative action, story, or scenario—it could be instructional (how to use/not use it), cultural (as part of a social ritual)—the item could be making something happen, or something could be happening to it. Use as many other objects/people as you like to create this scene.

Edit your images to one outcome per photographic instruction. How does the meaning or feeling of your object shift between these different modalities of photography? Which style of photography serves your item best? Why?

We are so used to viewing, capturing, and sharing images every day that the nuances of how we choose to frame the things we photograph can often feel automated. This exercise frames and re-frames a single object through different modalities of photography to explore the ways in which the camera shows us how to see and feel the things around us.

bad images

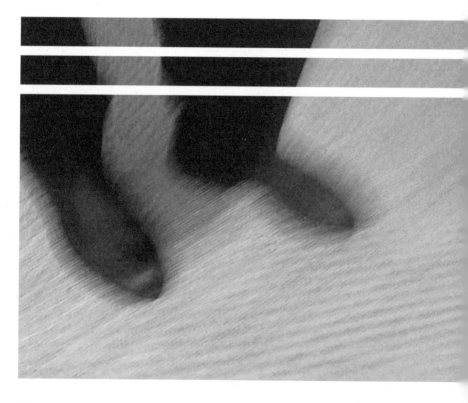

Use fashionable objects (with or without a model) as the subject of these experiments.

Use bad cameras: take a photo using non-cameras, such as a photocopier/scanner, the scan function on a phone app, a drone, or a webcam.

Deteriorate your image: take a photo (or work with a fashion image you have found) and put it through filters of deterioration. These can be analogue or digital. For instance, you can zoom in as far as you can to the image file. You can decrease (or increase) an image's resolution/quality using a photo editing program. Use an AI image generator.

Download the image or send it to someone over and over so that its resolution deteriorates. Experiment with the repetition of these processes or invent your own process of deterioration.

Pirate an image: print the image out, then take a photo of the print out. Re-photograph it on a screen. Photocopy it over and over.

Use filters: obstruct the image with glass objects or windows. Take a photo in the dark or oversaturate the image with extreme light.

Create bad compositions: disrupt the frame of your image through intentionally bad or awkward compositions. Photobomb your image. Set up a composition very far away and then zoom in. Take a photo upside-down whilst running or from a moving vehicle. Take the camera setting to an extreme: make your image out of focus or focus on the wrong feature in the image.

The poor image is a copy in motion. Its quality is bad, its resolution substandard. As it accelerates, it deteriorates. It is a ghost of an image, a preview, a thumbnail, an errant idea, an itinerant image distributed for free, squeezed through slow digital connections, compressed, reproduced, ripped, remixed, as well as copied and pasted into other channels of distribution. –Hito Steyerl (2009)[1]

The high production, smooth, and composed texture of a fashion image has become a characteristic facade. Its aesthetics of desire have an active role in the production and consumption of fashion; this is what *sells* the composition of fashionable items within its frame. This exercise asks you to explore and question these tendencies by making images that are bad, 'poor', or deficient in some way and thus at odds with the expensive and high-production formal qualities of the fashion image.

1   Hito Steyerl, 'In Defense of the Poor Image,' *e-flux journal*, no.10 (November 2009). www.e-flux.com/journal/10/61362/in-defense-of-the-poor-image/

Note: This exercise was developed as part of the Bachelor of Fashion (Design) (Honours) curriculum in the School of Fashion and Textiles at RMIT University, Melbourne.

garment
photo filter

This exercise uses garments or fabrics as a functional part of image creation. It suggests using a fashion object or fabric as a filter through a method of superimposition. The goal of this exercise is to explore the alternative functionality and potential of garments to create images.

1. Select a photo of a figure or clothed body and print it in colour or black and white.

2. Find and catalogue as many transparent or semi-transparent fabrics or garments as possible, in the colour of your choice. Note the composition of each fabric.

3. Hold the selected photo against a window or a bright surface, such as a lamp.

4. Cover it with the chosen fabric.

5. Take a picture. Play with the light and the overlapping of the fabrics.

6. Compare the original photo with the photos created using fabrics as filters. How does the fabric or garment change the feeling, mood, or meaning of the photo?

Recategorizing colour

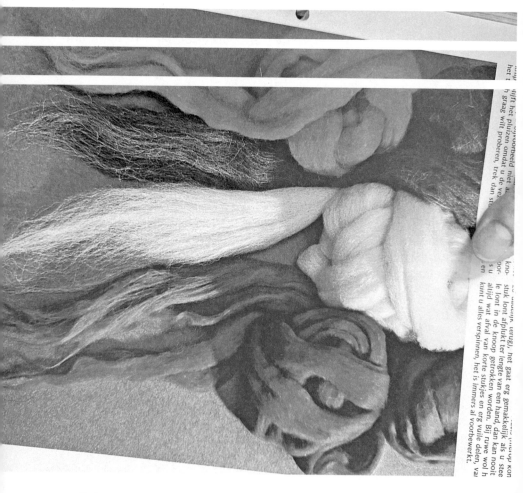

Select a set of colours using novel and improvised methods. This could include using the masking or eyedropper tools in Photoshop, photography hacks, digital and manual layering, experimenting with the effects of light on different surfaces, generating colours from AI prompts, or any other technique. Do not apply a theme; do not apply your personal taste. Grab at colours impulsively.

Then:

1. Apply a descriptor to each colour. Your word(s) may suggest sense, movement, permanence, transience, personhood, the metaphysical, or something else.

2. Give each colour a speculative era. This could be down to the minute or as broad as a millennia.

3. Notice your own emotional response to each colour. What is this response informed by?

4. Consider all existing associations with one of these colours. For example, what is its association to the cultural? Colonial? Scientific? Poetic? Political? Mythical?

5. Consider existing names or categories for these colours. How do your new descriptors relate to these?

6. Now gather your newly-interpreted colours together to create palettes. In this task, imagine a colour palette as a mutable landscape of everything you've just considered. It can be a sequence, a system, a novel, an emotional rollercoaster. Build gestures, stratas, and iterative compositions with your colours. Edit mindlessly until you edit decisively. Bring all your descriptors and comparisons together. What new language is formed? What story is emerging from these palettes? And finally, how will you document these colour investigations?

The human eye can perceive around a million colours. We respond to them emotionally and culturally, yet our methods of categorizing them are often reductive and predefined. How much do our existing biases inform how we see, read, and interact with colour? In this exercise you will develop an alternative taxonomy of colour, where hue and pigment are rewritten in terms of language, feeling, speculation, memory, and future. You are not naming house paints or nail enamel— you are re-imagining your relationship with colour.

Fashion image questionnaire

Choose a fashion image from the internet or a magazine and print it (if it is not printed already). Subject it to the questionnaire below. (If you don't know the answer to a question, try to make it up).

1. What is this image about?
2. Who is the image for?
3. What's the most obvious thing you notice when you look at the image?
4. What's the least obvious thing you notice when you look at the image?
5. What makes it a fashion image?
6. If you fold the image in three, what can you see in the bottom part?
7. If you fold the image in six, what can you see in the right top corner?
8. Where was it taken?
9. Who paid for it?
10. What was the temperature when the image was taken?
11. What was the political climate?
12. What was the life expectancy of the image?
13. What was considered 'luxury' in the image?
14. Is this image 'poor'?
15. Is this image 'rich'?
16. How many people were involved in making the image?
17. If this image was a meal what would it be?
18. How would it taste?
19. How would it smell?
20. If you scan the image, does it look different?
21. If you rephotograph the image, does it look any different?
22. If you burn it, is it still an image?

This exercise aims to critically and poetically investigate fashion images' materiality, narratives, histories, values, and affects. It situates fashion in geographic and socio-political contexts and creates playful and critical forms of engagement with visual culture. It is informed by Hito Steyerl's essay 'In Defense of the Poor Image', reflecting on the condition of digital images in contemporary culture, and uses a questionnaire as a tool for poetic, abstract, and situated knowledge production.

Note This is an updated version of a questionnaire created in 2018 for critical fashion courses and workshops at UDK Berlin, Germany, and School of Form, Warsaw, Poland.

wearers past and present

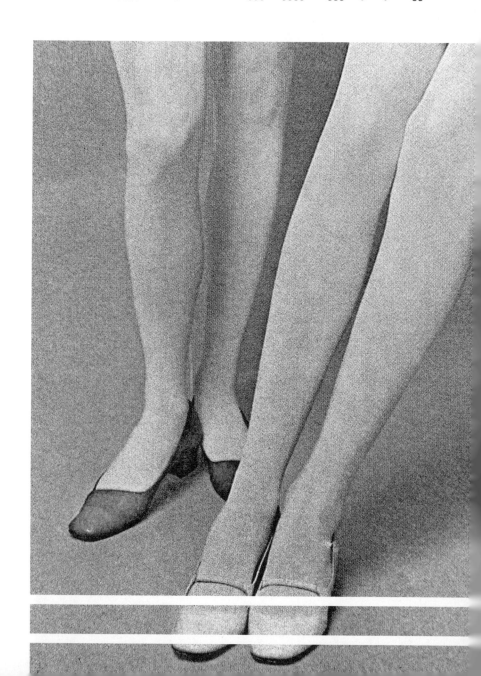

1. Choose a photograph that was taken at a different time from your own, that relates to your own history or background, and that pictures at least two people.
    Note: choose a picture that fascinates you, but that you don't know much about.

2. Dive into the details of the photograph. What garments are the people wearing? What are these garments made of? What are the objects, accessories, and buildings that the people are surrounded by?
    Note: visualize your examination—describe, draw, or annotate.

3. Take a deeper, imaginative dive. What would have been their favourite colours, food, garments, craft, games, friends, music, places?
    Note: visualize your imaginations—collect images, make drawings, or write notes.

4. Take a step towards reality: research the societal issues of the specific time and place that the photograph was taken. Do you see these issues reflected in the garments or accessories of the people in the picture?
    Note: choose a specific issue that fascinates you. Collect articles and pictures that give you insights into the topic.

5. Dive further into the realities of the past and take a small step towards your present. Research an artist, philosopher, sociologist, novelist, activist, or other that was influential in those times. What were their perspectives on the social issue at hand? How do you relate to the topic? Do you see it reflected in your garments, the objects that you surround yourself with?

Fashion often idealizes past events, shapes, styles, and communities. This exercise draws connections between a past wearer and you as a researcher by diving into materials, garments, and conditions that embody a societal issue.

The elusive vs. the everyday: a collection of found-object looks

'It might seem like, in the new world, clothes are nowhere to be found, but they are everywhere. In the desert, at the funeral home, in the garbage.'
– Margaux Williamson 2014[1]

This activity is best done in groups (of ideally two to six people).

1. Collect six images that you find inspiring. Try to look at the image itself as inspiration, not what (or who) is pictured. To make things interesting, you can limit your image search only to books you have at hand (or in your local library). Go off the beaten track of digital and analogue fashion media.

Don't use images from fashion magazines (especially not current issues). You can only work with images from books— avoid the algorithms and skip social media (Instagram and Pinterest in particular). Go to the 'Art' section of your local library and see what you find.

2. Combine your images as a group and discuss. Are there any common denominators? Doubles? Obvious opposites? Surprising combinations? Take your time to explore patterns in the images.

3. As a group, narrow down the images to about one third of the original collection (you can add other images if you wish). Take your time to put together various combinations. What makes a 'nice' or 'cohesive' collection of images? Discuss your choice.

4. Once you're happy with the group's selection, analyze again. Your new collection of images will serve as the mood board of a photo shoot. It must contain the following details: atmosphere, colour, texture, and shape.

5. Create an image based on your mood board using only the materials you have at hand. Do not use garments or large pieces of fabric. What can serve as the 'fashion' in your photoshoot? Look for anything that resembles the information on your moodnboard. Look at materials in a matter of colour, structure, shape, and/or appearance.

    You could work with a larger group of participants (between four and six) to make a complete editorial, including elements like casting, choice of location, photography (analogue, digital, smartphone, polaroid, etc.) based on their initial mood board. A smaller group of participants can make a 'lookbook' showing a small collection of their 'found-object'-looks inspired from the mood board.

This exercise looks at fashion beyond the garment by creating the elusive with the everyday. You are encouraged to look more critically and analytically at how an image serves as inspiration, and how literally anything can be translated into fashion.

1   In Sheila Heti, Heidi Julavits, Leanne Shapton et al., *Women in Clothes* (London: Penguin, 2014).

chance, systems, and design constraints

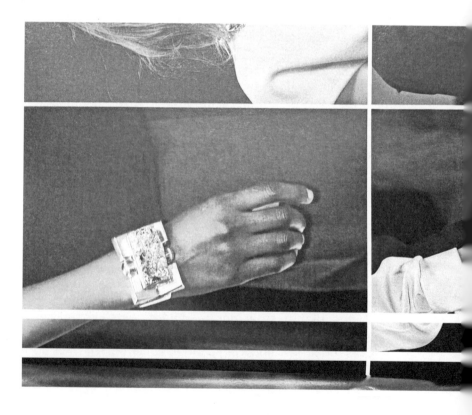

This exercise uses 'chance' to relinquish the control of the designer and prompt new garment compositions. Using dice, a series of rules is created and applied to a fashion magazine to generate reference images and a starting point for garment design.

1. Decide your source material. This activity uses a *Collezioni* magazine, but any fashion magazine (the older the better) can be used.

2. Create categories based on design elements. Start by deciding on six categories that might constitute a garment. For example, 'main fabric', 'details/trims', 'colour', 'silhouette', 'mood', etc. Number the categories one to six.

3. Get a marker and open your magazine. Starting from the beginning of the publication, working from numbers one to six, write a number, in order, on every fashion image featured in the publication. Take your time and be meticulous. Once you get to six you will need to start at one again, and so on.

4. Select twelve pages to work with. Roll two dice to get two numbers. These sets of numbers refer to the magazine page number you need to work with. For example, if die number one is four and die number two is seven, then your image reference is page forty-seven. Do this twelve times, noting the numbers.

5. Select the images you will work with. Open the page number you first rolled (in this example, page forty-seven). Roll one die. The number that appears tells you which image to use. For example, if five is rolled, and there are three images on the page that have this number, then you are working with these three images. Do this until you have six images. Label these six images 'one-a' to 'six-a'.

6. Repeat steps four and five until you have another six images. Label these 'one-b' to 'six-b'.

7. Place all sets of images together in their pairs. You now have twelve pairs of images as starting points to design.

8. Next, roll the dice for each of these image pairs so that each one corresponds to one of your chosen categories (there should be only one pair per category, if you repeat a number, roll again). Use these design constraints to produce a new design; you can either create a collage with the images or sketch from the original images. Stick to the originals and embrace the awkwardness of compositions you come up with.

digging

Fashion's newness is never new; it continually self-references and reaches back into the past. The study of fashion history is both systematic and interpretive; it narrates the present as much as it does the past. Exercises in the theme of 'Digging Deep' explore new ways for fashion to engage with history and counter its historical imbalances.

Many of these exercises challenge fashion's history and the colonial effects of such systems of power by resurfacing and sharing alternative cultural and social perspectives. Noorin Khamisani's 'Decolonizing Fashion Design, Discovering Lost Histories' addresses historical imbalances through connecting with local fashion or textile cultures and traditions. Marco Pecorari's 'Objects in Trouble' rethinks museum collections as representing 'ideologies of privilege, class distinction, and exploitation'.

'Digging Deep' exercises examine the supply chain involved in the production of the garments we wear. Anika Kozlowski's 'Look at Your Labels', for instance, asks us to trace the origins of our garments on a map. And Harriette Richards' 'Wardrobe Transparency' assigns us the uncomfortable but necessary task to 'rethink how fashion is valued by encouraging engagement with the complexity of supply chains and the challenges of determining where, how, and by whom our garments are made'.

Exercises in this theme also examine and reflect on the material artifacts of fashion, often on a detailed level. Ruby Hoette's 'Unpicking Garments and Systems' asks us to deconstruct a garment along its seam-lines as a metaphor 'for the unravelling or reversing of the mechanisms that constitute conventional fashion practices and production processes'. Gabriele Monti's 'Exercises on the Basis of a Study Collection' asks us to create our own archive of garments to reflect on their material properties as artifacts for storytelling. Nicole K. Rivas' 'The Social Life of Fashion Objects' is a method in contemporary archaeology looking at the life-cycle of the material artifacts of fashion.

an exercise in writing Hybrid criticism

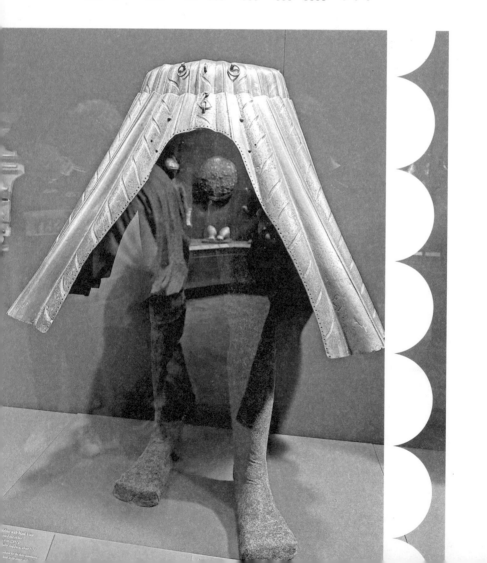

Choose an example of a project or practice that seems to mix the registers of art and fashion. This can be, for example, an artwork, exhibition, or product. Putting form aside, explore the following criteria of analysis: production, distribution, and exchange. Write sentences responding to each of the following points:

1. Who is (are) the author(s)?

2. How is it made – and by whom?

3. Is it unique, or a multiple?

4. Is it worn, used, or considered 'use-less'?

5. What is its lifespan?

6. How does it circulate in culture – online, in galleries, in shops, or somewhere else?

7. Is it for sale, and if so, who is selling and buying it?

8. Which institutions and museums would (or would not) collect and preserve it and why?

Compile your answers and integrate them into a short piece of criticism. Finally, re-evaluate your example. Has your perspective changed?

How to be a productive critic

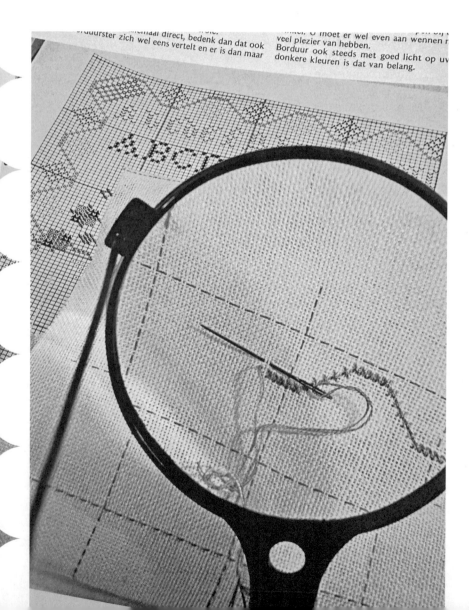

We live in difficult times filled with uncertainties about a shared future. Critics need to embrace a caring, encouraging, and supportive attitude in order to be productive and allow seeds to be sown for growing towards this unknown future. In other words, productive critics need to embrace new approaches—ones that do not, for example, denounce or denigrate the artist's/designer's/creative's work but seek to listen to their vision with a caring attitude, as mothers listen to their children.

Listen to their project carefully.

Imagine what will happen and enjoy it!

Decolonizing Fashion Design, Discovering Lost Histories

The following exercise aims to decolonize the study of
fashion by identifying, writing about, and uncovering little
known or lost fashion histories. The exercise proposes a
collaboration with sources or 'bearers' of knowledge (such
as a fashion archive) in a region underrepresented in current
fashion discourse. Such collaborations counter the cultural
appropriation that is rife in the fashion industry and connect
with varied fashion traditions in a more meaningful way.

Find a local fashion or textile culture or tradition that
is disappearing or underrepresented, perhaps even
undocumented.

Study (after having sought permission) the textile technique,
the colours, the ways of wearing, the stories of someone
who 'bears the knowledge'.

Document your findings, considering the best approach—a
combination of different media such as drawings,
photographs, videos, and interviews could all play a part.

Share the story you have discovered. Make it accessible to
others and perhaps even use it as the starting point for your
own design project.

This is not a straightforward process. As you embark on
this project, take care to reflect on your role (through, for
example, a reflective journal) in the process of engaging,
working with, and sharing underrepresented cultural
practitioners and forms.

Mapping ethnograph- ic fragments

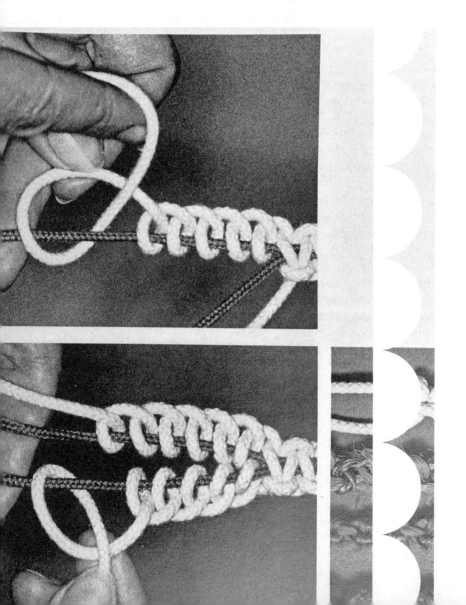

> The clothing of the rulers on the Shona and their followers was very different from that of their people. ...most wore the unusual dress of the wealthy Muslims of the East African coastal cities, a cloth from their middles to their feet, tucked in around the waist, and often another cloth worn around their shoulders and hanging down as a cloak. The really wealthy had their clothes so long that they dragged on the ground and thus wore away: conspicuous consumption in a Shona society. Men wore their hair as long as possible...the most popular fashion was for the hair to be arranged in horn-like shapes, the more the better. The women wore similar clothes from waist to calf, with heavy copper bangles from there to their feet...some of the richest people wore silks, damasks, satins and cloth of gold, often embroidered or decorated with ribbons, while the less well-off people wore imported Indian cottons, often dyed in stripes.[1]

This text fragment is from a country still defined by a line drawn in 1884, currently calling itself Zimbabwe. Such fragments found in archives of the long-past (900–1750) are a selection of fragments that challenge our and others' ideas of who we have been told we should be. The purpose of this activity is to destabilize ethnographic constructs related to notions of indigenousness.

Read the above fragment a few times.

Highlight words and/or phrases that raise your eyebrows.

On a separate page, sketch out the images that come to mind and that you associate with the text.

Embellish your sketches with words or phrases from the text, as you see fit.

Repeat this activity with other ethnographic passages of text.

1   David N. Beach, *The Shona and Zimbabwe, 900–1850: An Outline of Shona History* (Gweru, Zimbabwe: Mambo Press, 1980) 98.

The moral economy of fashion

The exercise can be done as an individual or in a group.

You will need: a pen, paper, pair of scissors, glue, and access to traditional and social fashion media (either in print or via a digital platform).

Add two headings to your sheet of paper: 'good' and 'bad'.

Start exploring various fashion media platforms you have access to. Find illustrations of codes of conduct or attitudes, values, and practices—both in their visual and written discourses—that are deemed 'good practice/behaviour/ways of thinking' by the dominant fashion culture. Note these under your heading 'good'.

Do the same for attitudes, values, and practices that are deemed 'bad' by the dominant fashion culture. Note these under the heading 'bad'.

Try to find patterns and trends of overarching themes under each of the headings.

Now contemplate whether you consider these codes of conduct as a guide for your own behaviour. In other words, do you believe that engaging in the codes of conduct demonstrated in the mapping of 'good' and 'bad' in the industrial fashion system make you a better person?

Focus on two patterns you have identified in this process. For example: 'beauty'. Assume that you allocated instances of 'white slenderness' to the 'good' side of your paper. Think through whether (racialized) 'beauty' is, according to you, in fact part of morality? Do you believe the fashion industry when it turns 'beauty' into a moral lifestyle choice?

Contemplate or discuss in a group 'who' or 'what' is being served by the moral boundaries you have found in fashion media's discourse.

Philosopher Michael J. Sandel (2012) characterizes contemporary society by saying that 'a market society is a way of life in which market values seep into every aspect of human endeavour'.[1] In a neoliberal-leaning political landscape, fashion has become a moral economy in which attitudes, values, and lifestyle choices are increasingly viewed as individual ethical choices. These moral boundaries allow individuals who consume at a slower pace or who invest in the upkeep of their looks to be perceived as 'better' people. This exercise thinks through the moral boundaries that are marketed to us by luxury and mass market fashion. It asks you to look at how morality plays out in the industrial fashion system and to what extent the industrial system's view on 'the good' is in line with your own personal moral convictions.

1   Michael Sandel, *What Money Can't Buy: The Moral Limits of Markets* (New York: Farrar, Strauss & Giroux, 2012), 13.

objects in trouble: rethinking fashion museum collections

In this exercise, you are asked to explore these issues through the study of an 'object in trouble' conserved in any Western-based fashion museum collection.

Select an object from a museum collection and propose a critical and alternative interpretation of it.

Try to move beyond canonical interpretations and narratives based on celebrity culture, authorship, and myth creation; show the complex problems behind the object.

Highlight the complexities behind the artefact, focusing on material evidence. Connect this to issues of the discursive construction of race, diversity, globalization, and national identity.

Use secondary sources (historical writings, poems, films, academic books and articles, music, etc.) to find alternative ways to present the 'troubles' that this object enables.

Propose a new interpretation (for example, an exhibition proposal, a performance, a publication, a diorama, a film) connecting the secondary sources with the 'object in trouble', in order to surpass its 'traditional' interpretation (and the museum's indexing) and expand the current discourse on fashion museology.

In recent years, increasing attention has been given to issues of decolonization, institutional racism, and cultural appropriation in relation to both the fashion industry and fashion museums. Museum collections, in particular, have been at the centre of the discussion as they often embody ideologies of privilege, class distinction, and exploitation. This is also the case for fashion museums, as collections of garments have sometimes historically been the repository of the fashion industry's exclusivity. The collecting and exhibition-making of these institutions tends to reinforce existing normative storytelling rather than problematize or critically appraise fashion discourses.

exercises on a study collection

Select two to three garments or fashion objects from your wardrobe (or from that of a parent, friend, or relative) or from second-hand stores. These garments form the beginning of your 'study collection'.

Carefully classify the garments in your study collection: document each with a detailed condition report and technical description of the construction and material of each object. The richness of your descriptions will be the basis for the next step.

After studying your garments, consider the following as starting points for design:

- Consider how your objects can be performed socially or critically.
- Replicate significant parts of the original garments.
- Pattern-make in reverse, starting from an existing garment.
- Deconstruct and reassemble the objects to form new ones.
- Starting from the object descriptions, choose keywords and design an exhibition.

A 'study collection' is a collection of garments that can be studied in detail, handled, and dissected. Unlike the museum collection, which is protected by strict standards of conservation, or images, which do not give you a material sense of a garment, a study collection can become raw material to explore the theoretical and technical postulates of fashion design. This activity forms a collective 'study collection'; it can be done individually or with a group of people.

The social life of fash- ion objects

Find a subject to interview. This could be a friend, friend of a friend, colleague, or family member.

Have your subject choose an object to discuss from their personal archives. This object must be inherited, second-hand, a hand-me-down, family heirloom, or kept with the intention of passing it onto future generations.

Complete a condition report of the object.

Take a photo of the object.

Ask the subject the following questions:
- What object have you chosen and why?
- How did you acquire it?
- How often is this object worn?
- What is the fondest memory you have with this object?
- How will this object be used in the future?
- What is the object's connection to your personal upbringing and culture?
- Do you consider this object a part of your material biography? Explain.

Record the interview. These questions are intended as a guideline—you can also write your own questions. Let the interview evolve into a conversation and a story about the object.

Take a portrait of the subject wearing the object.

Ask the subject whether they have any documentation material of the object's previous owner (such as family photographs, films, letters, etc.). Make sure to document these artefacts by recording, scanning, or photographing them in addition to note taking observations.

This activity unveils the narrative of an object's lifecycle. A wearer's 'material biography' explores how artefacts are used, lived in, displayed, and experienced in constructing self-identity. An object's provenance reveals its context within contemporary archaeology.

Look at your labels

Split into groups of two to five people. Record the manufacturing country identified on the labels of all the garments worn by all group members.

Using Google Maps, pin on the map the countries where the group members' garments were made.

Make a list of all the countries identified.

Tabulate how many garments are made in each country identified.

Discuss the following questions:
- Where are the majority of your garments made?
- How do you feel about the results (surprise, shame, nothing)?
- What are three things that the labels do not tell us about our garments?
- What type of information should appear on a garment label and/or would you like to see when evaluating a garment for purchase?
- What can you do to reduce the impact (or increase the positive impact) of your wardrobe?

Western fashion 'brand names' are often manufactured offshore in countries/regions with low wages and limited environmental regulation, in particular in East and South Asia. However, most of the garments made in these regions are bought and sold in affluent nations such as Europe, North America, and Japan. The aim of this activity is to bring awareness about what the information on a garment label is telling us and what it is not telling us. Identifying what information we would like to see provides insight into what we value. Identifying what we value can be helpful in determining the 'sustainability' of a product. Determining the 'sustainability' of a product is subjective and nuanced, given the complexity of producing, using, and disposing of fashion products and the abundance of sometimes dubious information on the topic.

Embodied material processes

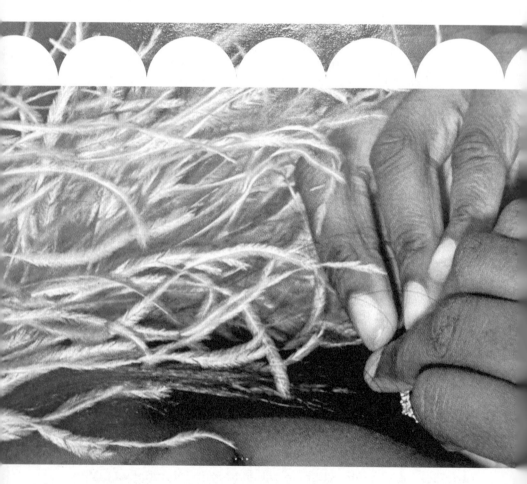

Select a garment from your wardrobe.

Identify all the materials used in its construction by looking at the care label. Pay close attention to all aspects such as trimmings (don't forget dyes).

Using the library or internet, break each material in the garment down to its raw materials. Go back to the beginning—right back to the land in which the material was grown or extracted. Select three different raw materials from your list.

For each material, find out:
- What is it (a plant, animal, mineral, other)?
- What is the material's average lifecycle? In other words, is it reproduced annually or does it take centuries or millennia to develop?
- Where is it mainly produced? Is it naturally forming or introduced?
- When did it start being produced there and why? For iron ore, this will reveal lengthy time periods and tectonic activity. For agricultural products, this may show patterns of colonization and land clearing.
- How is it produced/extracted (for example, through mining or harvesting)?
- What other materials are required for its production?

Using a roll of paper, develop a timeline for each material, ensuring the scale of temporal distance remains consistent.

Add any geographic information to the timeline using maps, images, and significant events (species introduction, geologic activity, etc.).

Identify where you, the wearer, are situated on this timeline. What reciprocal times, events, and places are you embodying?

The objects of fashion are developed from recognizable materials—fabric, zippers, thread—derived from the processing and refinement of plants, animals, minerals, iron ore, and petrochemicals. Some of these materials are the result of ancient geologic processes, while others occur annually through agricultural practices, often in areas that are well-suited to production but are not the species' native habitat. This exercise reveals the places we embody through our garments and the spatio-temporal processes of production and extraction inherent to the materials of these garments.

wardrobe trans- parency

Think of the item of clothing you purchased most recently.

Why did you purchase it?

Did you think about where/how it was made, or about who made it?

Can you find out:
- Where it was made: in what country, town, factory?
- Who made it: whose hands touched the garment in its production?
- What it is made of: which type of material, fibre, or cloth?
- Where and how the fabric was made: woven, dyed, processed?
- What thread was used and where this came from?
- Where the hardware (zippers, buttons, buckles, etc.) came from and who made these?
- What it was packaged in and how it was transported to you?
- Who was involved in the transportation and delivery: packing, shipping, logistics?

If you cannot find answers to some or all of these questions, what does this tell you?

Given what you have or have not been able to find out about where, how, and by whom this garment was made, do you think the price reflects its value? Why?

How does this information affect your understanding of a garment being 'good value'?

Prompted by the 2013 collapse of the Rana Plaza garment factory in Dhaka, Bangladesh, and the subsequent establishment of the Fashion Revolution activist movement, 'radical transparency' has become a fashionable ideal in recent years. This exercise asks all clothing-wearers to rethink how fashion is valued by encouraging engagement with the complexity of supply chains and the challenges of determining where, how, and by whom our garments are made.

unpicking garments and systems

Start by choosing a garment to work with (it can be something you no longer wear or something from a second-hand shop. Denim garments usually work very well).

Draw/sketch and photograph the garment as an entire object and close-up. Note any particular details and information on the labels, signs of wear, changes in fabric thickness, type or colour, and type of construction. Use an almost forensic approach to observe and document.

Choose a seam and begin to unpick it (noting the type of seam and stitching) until it is completely undone. Continue this process with the rest of the seams, taking notes, sketches, and photographs as you work around the garment. Work slowly and methodically. Do not cut through any seams or construction elements—find ways to deconstruct so the pieces remain in their original shapes.

Collect any remnants of thread, fabric, or dust that emerge from the seams as you open them.

Once you have opened all the seams, lay out all the loose materials (fabric pieces, buttons, threads, etc.) on a table or floor space and photograph them from above. What do you notice about the new form(s) and shapes now that the garment is 'exploded' or deconstructed?

Using the material details discovered, map/diagram and/ or describe how your garment relates with or connects to modes of production and patterns of use that you are aware of in the fashion system. Where was the garment made and how? What type of finishing details or treatment does it have? What is the fabric composition? Is it 'good' or 'bad' quality? How much has it been worn? Add your own questions.

This method produces knowledge both at a material and systemic level. By dissecting, unpicking, or unravelling a garment along its original seam lines one becomes materially engaged with the garment in a very specific way. The act of 'un-making' gives a visceral experience of the materiality of the garment, an indirect connection with those involved in its conception and production, and a sense of the time and skill involved. It also enables a heightened understanding of the complexity of the fashion system functioning as a metaphor for the unravelling of the mechanisms that constitute pervasive fashion production processes. The resulting garment elements can be left loose or function as the material with which to start to construct new assemblages. Reassembling and reconfiguring these elements enables an alternative experience of the construction of fashion.

Unpicking garments along original seam-lines functions as a metaphor for the unravelling or reversing of the mechanisms that constitute conventional fashion practices and production processes. The activity requires time, focus, and curiosity, and places the emphasis on 'un-making' as a method of both knowledge and material production.

Note: This method has been developed and iterated in collaboration with Katherine May. It was part of the MA Fashion curriculum from 2013–2017 and since 2017 it has been an integral part of the Fashions & Embodiment Studio as part of the MA in Design: Expanded Practice at Goldsmiths, University of London.

our threads

1. Ground yourself in your research. Gather pictures/objects that relate to the categories below. Assemble these as a scrapbook/short film/visual poem. Make sure the method you use does not stifle your creativity.

   Where you are from. What makes your country itself? For instance, what makes Nigeria Nigeria? What are some known facts, languages, tourist attractions, and so forth, that are specific to your country? What are the things that are unique to that place? What do/did you enjoy about this place? You may document food, celebrations, ways of dressing, habits, language, etc.

   Your family. Who are the people you consider family? What do/did you do together? What do/did you enjoy most about spending time with these people? What is the story behind your family name/family heritage?

   You. How would you describe yourself? What do you enjoy doing?

2. Write a short story that you feel encapsulates the assemblage(s) you made.

3. Design a garment based on your story. Consider repurposing materials (this could be words, images, fabric, or other media) that were part of your research. For fabrics, source from garments you no longer wear or from those discarded by fashion companies.

The aim of this activity is to engage in remembrance based on the Nigerian Yorùbá practice of storytelling, Àló (ah-lawh), which could translate to 'folktales'. The storyteller starts a story, during which a song is sung. The listeners sing along, and then the story ends. The cycle continues until the storyteller has told all the stories they wanted to tell. Through these stories, elders teach us about life; valuable lessons are embedded in each narrative. It is up to the listener to actively listen and follow these lessons. In this exercise, you develop your own folktale and engage in the act of remembering—telling your stories through garment design.

sourcing
re-sourci

Existing systems of fashion production contain hidden inequities and environmental damage, not to mention being geared towards over-consumption and -production. 'Sourcing and Re-sourcing' looks at radical and environmentally sustainable ways of resourcing materials for fashion production through reuse and grass-roots making. For instance, Annie Wu's exercise 'Source the Source' challenges you to be your own supply chain by making your garments from scratch, including producing all the materials and tools you might need for their construction. Could you do it?

At the core of both fashion and textiles is their origin point—the materials from which they are produced. Once those materials, be they wool, flax, linen, polyester, nylon, etc., are dyed and processed, they move so far from their origin point that they cannot return. Fashion cycles continue to change and leave behind the problem of how to deal with fashion's overwhelming waste, which seems to continually plague us. Another way we can shift fashion's value system around 'newness' and 'renewal' is by revaluing what is left behind in the production of fashion. Georgia McCorkill, Rachael Cassar, Anouk Beckers, and Claire Myers offer us exercises for reusing and, more importantly, revaluing discarded, or no longer wanted, garments. Rachael Cassar's exercise 'Debris Assemblage' reflects on the waste debris of a studio practice. Other exercises that guide the reader through methods of re-use include Claire Myers' 'Re-making' exercise, Georgia McCorkill's 'Ideational Stocktake', and Anouk Beckers' 'Make Your own Modular Garments'.

source
and create
Holiday

This exercise is for those about to relocate to a new location for work or study, on holiday in a new city, or visiting their family for a few weeks. Arrive with only what you are wearing and no additional wearables in your luggage. Source and create all the necessary garments needed during your trip by sourcing materials only from the new location. Materials can be found, bought in a store, donated, or upcycled from existing garments—but all must be from the new location.

make your own modular garments

You will need:
- Two T-shirts.
- Scissors.
- Twenty ribbons (each should be at least fifteen centimeters long).
- A tool to attach the ribbons to your T-shirt. There are different ways to do this: knotted through, stitched (hand or machine stitch), using staples or studs, etc.

1. Disassemble your T-shirt by cutting the following seams:
   - Armholes: you should end with four 'loose' sleeves.
   - Side seams: both left and right, this is to disassemble the front and back panels of your T-shirt.
   - Shoulder seams.

2. You should now have eight garment pieces: four sleeves, four body-parts (i.e. the fronts and the backs of the T-shirts).

3. Attach the ribbons. The placement of the ribbons is important for your modular system, since this is the key to attaching all your garment pieces. It's important that the spots for your ribbons (marked with x in the drawing) match your other pieces. You can use the drawing below as a starting point but adjust to your own needs (in case you would like fewer or more ribbons).

4. Start joining your garment pieces to create the new T-shirts. Your design can change over time by reassembling the pieces, for instance, if you want to 'refresh' your T-shirt, you can add new garment pieces to the modular garments system by disassembling another T-shirt or exchanging pieces with others. Enjoy wearing your modular garment.

Make your own modular garments using what you can find in your wardrobe at home. This exercise starts with a T-shirt, but you can do this with any other garment. When you are finished with this exercise, you can start wearing your own modular garments or exchange pieces with someone else.

Note: This exercise was developed from the open-source modular garments system JOIN Collective founded in 2019 by Anouk Beckers.

re-making

This exercise aims to create innovative, zero waste forms through the deconstruction and reconstruction of an existing garment archetype—the T-shirt.

1. Find five T-shirts of a similar size at a charity store.

2. Cut the T-shirts along each of their seams until each T-shirt becomes four individual flat pieces: two sleeves, a front, and a back.

3. Begin by draping a panel onto an area of a mannequin or your own body where it is not usually located. Consider turning the piece upside down or sideways. For example: a sleeve as a bodice; the head hole as waistline or armhole; or the front and back panels as sleeves.

4. Using pins, begin to add more panels to the garment, building onto it around the mannequin or body. Place the other pieces in locations they wouldn't usually sit while working them together like a puzzle.

5. Consider pleats, tucks, darts, and gathers to fit stubborn panels together or to create shaping. Try to avoid trimming and if a cut is necessary, do so in a way where the off-cut becomes a new panel.

6. Think about the way you finish the T-shirts: overlocked hems and sleeves, neck ribbing—how could these finishes remain intact and enhance the new garments?

7. Pin together six garment propositions and photograph as you work through the iterative experimental process.

    Change up how you combine the pieces. For example: a garment using all ten sleeves; a garment using only front and back panels; or a garment using every single panel of all five T-shirts.

meaningful deconstruc- tion

Find a piece of woven textile with some wear and tear—be it an old scarf with a pulled thread or a table cloth with a hole.

1. Begin at the point of wear and tear.

2. Be inspired by this point. Could you undo the weave to create a new pattern? Could you create emptiness within the textile to breathe new life into it?

3. Identify a deconstructive technique. For example: burning, unravelling, or bleaching.

4. Sketch out a new pattern that can be done with this technique.

5. Apply the technique. In the case of unravelling, you may start with a tweezer to unravel the weft.

6. Attempt to reintroduce the unravelled threads back into the textile as embroidery or embellishments.

Can we add value through the act of removal? This exercise seeks to reframe how designers upcycle objects through acts of slowness and tenderness and through cultural craft knowledge.

ideational stocktake

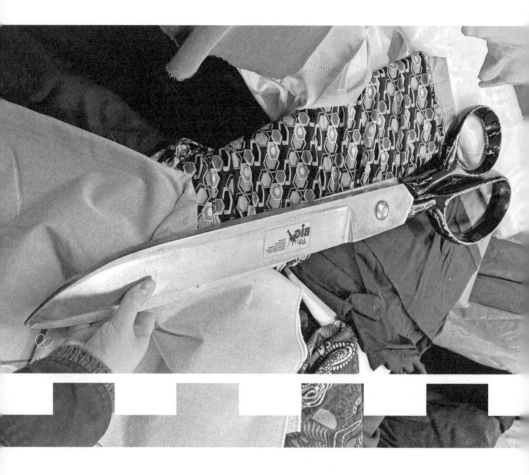

This exercise regards the materiality of disused textiles as the basis for design inspiration and as a concept for fashion outcomes. Three active and creative steps—'Collecting', 'Sorting', and 'Noticing'—help make sense of materials and discover ways that they can be fashioned into new forms.

1. Collecting. There is an abundance of discarded, remnant, or second-hand textiles available for repurposing. If your

intent is to develop solutions that use the most waste possible, then locating large quantities of similar materials is important. Consider the motivations behind your choice of materials, including personal inclination, nostalgia, or the pleasure of working with certain fibres.

Think creatively about where you can source discarded materials. It is simple to purchase second-hand garments from opportunity/thrift shops, but you might also contact designers and manufacturers to see what they have available in their waste stream.

2. Sorting. Sorting is a generative activity done according to one criterion, then repeated according to another. Think about the 'elements of design' in forming the criteria. For example, you could sort according to:
    - Size.
    - Shape.
    - Colour.
    - Material.
    - Texture.
    - Drape or handle.

    Let sorting be creative. Lay out materials in collages or jigsaw puzzles. Pin them to a wall, lay them on the floor, or hang them up. Full garments can be sorted through slow unpicking: revealing one part of the garment at a time, stopping to document and notice. Then, unpick the whole and sort by component pieces, such as linings, outers, or sleeves.

3. Noticing. Record your visual and tactile observations in your sketchbook. How much material do you now have? What shapes and patterns are made by the materials? At a tactile level, is the material bulky, light, or sheer? Slippery, slubbed, smooth, crisp? What feelings or impressions are evoked through the gathered materials?

    From here, you could design a form using your materials. Notice which 'elements of design' could become the focus of your design. For example, noticing the triangular shapes of fabric remnants leads to reflection on how those remnants might explore repetition or radiation, in turn driving a garment's form.

debris assemblage

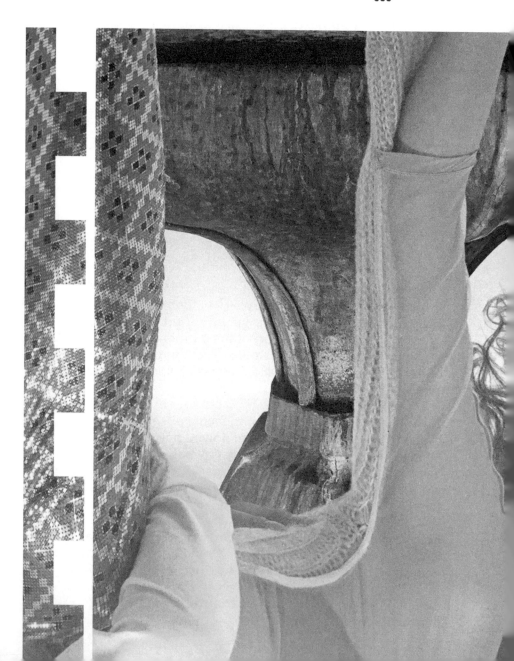

1. Go to your work space and look down at the floor. Do you see any remnants of a past production? Single, random beads, material scraps, clumps of threads?

2. Gather these components. Be inclusive. Everything is valuable.

3. Find a surface such as a box or a tray.

4. Start to assemble the workshop debris in the box. Spend some time moving these debris leftovers around, like moving food around on a plate. Let them communicate with each other.

5. Conduct a surface reading: touch the debris, take note of its material qualities, reflect on the material composition. Photograph your materials and take notes on how they feel.

6. Start to stitch an assemblage together, any way you know how. This should be a slow act of isolating individual 'bits' and responding to their material properties.

7. Take your assemblage to a body. Start to use this as a design prompt for a textile surface. Design into and around this assemblage by constructing different possibilities using fabrics. All decisions must honour this materiality.

This method re-evaluates discarded materials by re-using them within the creative process. Reuse, through this frame, provides a means of critique and resistance to wastefulness, hyper-materialism, and excess.

wearing your waste

and boil.

In this exercise, unwanted textiles from friends are collected and dyed with daily food waste (such as peels and seeds of fruits and vegetables).

1. Collect some unwanted textile pieces in light shades. Your collection may include garments, tea towels, bed linens, an old turban, etc. Plant-based fabrics (such as cotton, linen, and ramie) are recommended as these will hold the natural dye best. Ensure these are clean and, if necessary, wash them.

2. Collect peels and pits of vegetables and fruits you consume. If you are working on your own, this may take several weeks; otherwise, reach out to your community to speed up the process. You may also use coffee and tea. Wash and dry the pits and skins of avocados. Place vegetable peels (such as those of onions and carrots) in a sealed box in the fridge until you are ready to dye. These plant materials will contribute to your dye bath.

3. You will need a large saucepan with a lid, water, and some kitchen salt; the latter will act as mordant. Stainless steel vessels and wooden spoons work best. Place your scraps in the pot with water to cover and add three spoons of salt. Cover and leave it to boil for a minimum of an hour. Check regularly and mix gently from time to time.

4. Soak your fabric in clean water and place the fabric in an empty large vessel. Carefully strain the scraps liquid into the vessel with your fabric; the coloured liquid should submerge your fabric. Cover and let the dye do its work for at least an hour and up to twenty-four hours, depending on the intensity of the result you seek.

5. Rinse the dyed fabric and let it dry—repeat steps three and four as many times as you like with different materials. You might want to use this material to create a garment or a piece for your home.

Note: My series of works titled *Penser, Manger, Partager* [Think, Eat, Share] directly influenced this exercise and employs home materials.

Nearby infinities

Wonder and innovation are within our reach. This exercise allows us to discover the infinite, transformative potential of materials and objects that are already around us, or that we have simply discarded. It trains awareness and attention and proposes 'deep recycling' as a way of making fashion.

1. Take six unused or dried tea bags. Observe them closely.

2. Gently take them apart so that all the components are separated (staple, string, paper label, paper bag, loose tea).

3. Put the different materials per category in front of you and observe them very carefully. Look, feel, hear, smell, and taste each one.

4. Experiment with ways to reassemble these parts (or a selection of them) into new materials or new forms. Push yourself to work only with these materials while using only a minimum of external aids (glue, needle and thread, stapler,...). Play!

5. Repeat this process at least five times; each time, with six new tea bags. You will get the most out of this exercise if you continue to the point where you think you have exhausted your possibilities.

temporary loss

Wear worn-down clothes.
Borrow clothes.
Share a wardrobe.
Don't buy any new clothes for three years.
Travel for ten days with a handbag only.
Refrain from material pleasures, e.g. take a cold shower
instead of a hot one.

You can rid yourself of many useless things among those that
disturb you, for they lie entirely in your imagination; and you
will then gain for yourself ample space by comprehending
the whole universe in your mind, and by contemplating the
eternity of time, and observing the rapid change of every part of
everything, how short is the time from birth to dissolution, and
the illimitable time before birth as well as the equally boundless
time after dissolution [...][1]

Reconsider the sociological meanings in material goods and
establish alternative ones by experiencing the temporary loss of
current season fashion.

1   Marcus Aurelius, *Meditations* (London: Dover
     Publications, 1997), 72.

source the source

Recreate a garment by making everything you need for every step of the construction. This might include thread, fibre, or any tools you would like to use.

Choose a garment (it might be one from your wardrobe or one from a magazine) and try to recreate this garment from scratch. You are your own supply chain and supplier: you must create your own thread or think of a way of creating a garment without seams, weave/knit/compress/felt your own fabric, and add colour. Every tool you use must be made by you or be naturally sourced. Document each step of this process with photographs and videos. Exhibit this together with the original garment.

Imagining and Dreaming

pp. 22–23
Connections
Martine Rose

pp. 24–25
Fashion Relic
PAGEANT (Amanda Cumming & Kate Reynolds)
Vries, de Femke. *Dictionary Dressings*. Eindhoven: Onomatopee, 2016.
Porter, Charlie. *What Artists Wear*. London: Penguin Books, 2021.
Heti, Sheila, Heidi Julavits, Leanne Shapton & 639 others. *Women in Clothes*. London: Penguin Books, 2014.

pp. 26–27
Know Your Enemy
Valerie Lange
Lange, Valerie and Patz, Jana. 'Kritische Betrachtung rechter Mode aus der Perspektive des Modedesigns.' In *Rechte Angriffe-toxische Effekte*, edited by Elke Gaugele and Sarah Held, 93–102. Bielefeld: Transcript Verlag, 2021.

pp. 28–29
Writing from a Garment's Perspective
Marieke Coppens
Lopate, Phillip. *The Art of the Personal Essay: An Anthology from the Classical Era to the Present*. Hamburg: Anchor, 1997.
Paustovsky, Konstantin. *Selected Stories*. Amsterdam: Fredonia Books, 2003.
Didion, Joan. *We Tell*

Ourselves Stories in Order to Live: Collected Nonfiction. Introduction by John Leonard. New York: Everyman's library, 2006.
MacGregor, Neil. *Living with the Gods: on Beliefs and Peoples*. New York: Vintage, 2018.

pp. 30–31
Ways of (Re)collecting
sihle sogaula
Bueis, Yolanda de los, Christoph Schwarz, Elisa Marchesini and Sarah Vanhee. *Untranslatables: A Glossary of Untranslatable Words*. Eindhoven: Onomatopee, 2009.

pp. 32–33
Ridicule Fashion Manners
Clemens Thornquist
Epictetus. *Enchiridion*. London: Dover Publications, 2004.

pp. 34–35
Not-Making
Marjanne van Helvert
Fisher, Mark. *Capitalist Realism, Is there no Alternative?* Winchester, Hampshire: John Hunt Publishing, 2009.

pp. 36–37
Anti-Engagement Strategy
Chinouk Filique de Miranda
Daniels, Dieter. 'Subversion as Strategy Today? Political Interventions.' In *Edition Digital Culture* 1. Oxfordshire, United Kingdom: CMV publishers, 2014. www.academia.edu/27444507/Dieter_Daniels_Subversion_as_

pp. 40–41
Body Evolutions
Julie Gork
Harbisson, Neil. 'I Listen to Colour.' Ted Talk. July 20, 2012. www.ted.com/talks/neil_harbisson_i_listen_to_color?language=en
Smelik, Anneke. 'Fractal Folds: The Posthuman Fashion of Iris van Herpen.' *Fashion Theory* 26, no.1 (2022): 5–26.
Vänskä, Annamari. 'How to Do Humans with Fashion: Towards a Posthuman Critique of Fashion.' *International Journal of Fashion Studies* 5, no. 1 (2018): 15–31.

pp. 42–43
Interspecies Collaborative Design
Daphne Mohajer va Pesaran
Williams, Nina. 'Waiting for Geotropic Forces: Bergsonian Duration and the Ecological Sympathies of Biodesign.' *Qualitative Inquiry* 28, no. 5 (2022): 486–495. www.journals.sagepub.com/doi/abs/10.1177/10778004211065803
Williams, Nina, and Carole Collet. 'Biodesign and the Allure of "Grow-Made" Textiles: an Interview with Carole Collet.' *GeoHumanities* 7, no. 1 (2021): 345–357. www.tandfonline.com/doi/full/10.1080/2373566X.2020.1816141?journalCode=rgeo20
Ginsberg, Alexandra Daisy, and Natsai Chieza. 'Other Biological Futures.' *Journal of Design and Science* (2018). www.jods.mitpress.mit.edu/otherbiologicalfutures

Going Outside

pp. 56–57
Intentional Noticing
Daphne Mohajer va Pesaran
Dumit, Joseph. 'Writing the Implosion: Teaching the World One Thing at a Time.' *Cultural Anthropology* 29, no. 2 (2014): 344–62. www.doi.org/10.14506/ca29.2.09.
Stewart, Kathleen. *Ordinary Affects*. Durham, NC: Duke University Press, 2007.
Tsing, Anna Lowenhaupt. *Arts of Living on a Damaged Planet: Ghosts and Monsters of the Anthropocene*. Minneapolis: University of Minnesota Press, 2017.
Wex, Marianne. *Let's Take Back Our Space: Female and Male Body Language as a Result of Patriarchal Structures*. Berlin, Germany: Frauenliteratur Verlag, 1979.

pp. 58–59
Radical Noticing
Kate Fletcher
Fletcher, Kate. *Wild Dress: Clothing & the Natural World.* Axminster: Uniform Books, 2019.

pp. 60–61
Notes on Globalized Fashion
Ferdinand Waas
Boehn Von, Max. *Die Mode.* Munich: F. Bruckmann KG, 1963.
Squire, Geoffry. *Dress Art and Society 1560–1970.* London: Studio Vista, 1974.
Klein, Ruth. *Lexikon der Mode.* Baden-Baden: Woldemar Klein Verlag, 1950.
Longoria, Julia, Gabrielle Berbey, and Alvin Melathe. 'The Case for Sweatpants.' Podcast February 18, 2021. www.wnyc-studios.org/podcasts/experiment/episodes/sweatpants
Wattig, Leander. 'ARTE-Doku: Die ganze Welt in einem Bild—Vermeers spätes Vermächtnis.' Documentary, 2021. www.leanderwattig.com/dokuliebe/allzeit-perlen/2021/die-ganze-welt-in-einem-bild-vermeers-spaetes-vermaechtnis/

pp. 62–63
Counter-Choreography
Aïcha Abbadi
Boyd, Andrew, ed. *Beautiful Trouble: A Toolbox for Revolution.* New York: OR Books.

pp. 64–65
Spending Time
Alessandra Vaccari & Marco Marino
Evans, Caroline and Alessandra Vaccari, eds. *Time in Fashion.* London-New York: Bloomsbury, 2020.
Fitterman, Robert. *Sprawl: Metropolis 30A.* Los Angeles: Make Now Press, 2010.
Goldsmith, Kenneth. *Uncreative Writing: Managing*

Language in the Digital Age. New York: Columbia University Press, 2011.
Koolhaas, Rem, Jens Hommert, and Michael Kubo (eds.). *Projects for Prada: Part 1.* Milan: Fondazione Prada, 2001.

pp. 66–67
G.U.C.C.I. (Genuine Unauthorized Clothing Clone Institute)
Abigail Glaum-Lathbury

pp. 68–69
Counter-Tools
Mikhail Rojkov
Lorde, Audre. 'The Master's Tools Will Never Dismantle the Master's House.' In *Sister Outsider: Essays and Speeches.* Trumansburg, NY: Crossing Press, 1984.
Von Busch, Otto. 'Engaged Design and the Practice of Fashion Hacking: The Examples of Giana Gonzalez and Dale Sko.' *Fashion Practice,* Vol. 1, no. 2 (2009): 163–185.

ROBAFLÖR

pp. 70–71
Pockets for Peace
Otto von Busch
Fromm, Erich. *The Art of Loving.* New York: Harper, 1956.

Scarry, Elaine. *The Body in Pain.* Oxford: Oxford University Press, 1985.
Stilgoe, John. *Outside Lies Magic.* New York: Walker & Company, 1998.

Using the Body

pp. 80–81
Body Exhibition
Paola Di Trocchio
Clark, Judith. 'Doppie Pagine: Not Spelling It Out.' *Fashion Theory* 10, no. 1–2 (2006): 259–277.
Cunningham, Bill. 'On the Street: Apart From the Crowd.' *The New York Times,* 27 March 1994.
Steele, Valerie. 'A Museum of Fashion Is More Than a Clothes-Bag.' *Fashion Theory* 2, no. 4 (1998): 327–335.

pp. 82–83
Covering
Ulrik Martin Larsen
The Hundertwasser Nonprofit Foundation. 'The Five Skins.' www.hundertwasser.com/en/applied-art/apa382_mens_five_skins_1975

pp. 86–87
Jewellery Hunting
Naoko Ogawa

pp. 88–89
Design for Moving Bodies
Todd Robinson
Laban, Rudolf. *The Mastery of Movement* (Fourth ed.). Plymouth, United Kingdom: Northcoate House, 1980.

Negrin, Llewellyn. 'Maurice Merleau-Ponty: The Corporeal Experience of Fashion.' In *Thinking Through Fashion: A Guide to the Key Theorists* edited by Agnès Rocamora and Anneke Smelik, 115. London, New York: I.B. Taurus, 2016.

Robinson, Todd. 'Body Styles: Redirecting Ethics and the Question of Embodied Empathy in Fashion Design.' *Fashion Practice* (2022). www.doi.org/10.1080/17569370.2022.2026048.

pp. 90–91
The Intersection of Body and Material
Laura Banfield

pp. 92–93
Designing from Movement
Linnea Bågander
Bågander, Linnea. 'Body Movement as Material: Designing Temporal Expressions.' Borås: Högskolan i Borås, Akademin för textil, teknik och ekonomi, 2021. www/hb.diva-portal.org/smash/record.jsf?pid=diva2%3A1510409&dswid=6391

Dean, Sally. 'Somatic Movement and Costume: A Practical Investigative Project.' *Journal of Dance & Somatic Practices* 3, no. 1 and 2 (2011): 167–182.

Fernandes, Ciane. *Moving Researcher: Laban/Bartenieff Movement Analysis in Performing Arts Education and Creative Arts Therapies*. London: Jessica Kingsley Publishers, 2015.

Schlemmer, Oskar. 'Man and Art Figure.' In *The Theater of the Bauhaus*, edited by Walter Gropius and Arthur Wensinger, 17–48. Baltimore, MD and London: Johns Hopkins University Press, [1925] 1996.

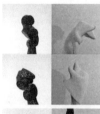

pp. 94–95
Unpacking the Memory of Garments
Sanem Odabaşı
Assmann, Jan, and John Czaplicka. 'Collective Memory and Cultural Identity.' *New German Critique* 65 (1995): 125–133.

Hunt, Carole. 'Worn Clothes and Textiles as Archives of Memory.' *Critical Studies in Fashion & Beauty* 5, no. 2 (2014): 207–232.

Proust, Marcel. *Swann's Way: In Search of Lost Time, Volume 1*. Vol. 1. New Haven, Connecticut: Yale University Press, 2013.

pp. 96–97
The Art Studio of the Mouth
Marie Hugsted
Brandt, Eva, Johan Redström, Mette Agger Eriksen, and Thomas Binder. *Xlab*. Denmark: Danish Design School Press, 2011.

Mouritsen, Ole G., and Klavs Styrbæk. *Tsukemono: Decoding the Art and Science of Japanese Pickling*. London: Springer Nature, 2021.

pp. 98–99
Soundscape of a Look
PAGEANT (Amanda Cumming & Kate Reynolds)
Echeverri, Maria. 'Essay: The Sound of Clothes.' *ShowStudio* item 5, October 9, 2013. www.showstudio.com/projects/the_sound_of_clothes/essay_the_sound_of_clothes

Knight, Nick. 'Fashion Film: Maison Martin Margiela.' *ShowStudio* item 13, April 20, 2006.

www.showstudio.com/projects/the_sound_of_clothes/fashion-film-maison-martin-margiela?autoplay=1

Cage, John and Knowles, Alison. *Notations*. New York: Something Else Press, 1969.

pp. 100–101
Sound to Wear
Vidmina Stasiulytė

pp. 102–103
Sensuous Description
Julie Gork
Findlay, Rosie. 'On the Delight of Fashion Words.' *The Conversation*. July 28, 2014. www.theconversation.com/on-the-delight-of-fashion-words-29732

Le Breton, David. 'Sensory Play, Wordplay: The Common Sense of Sensing.' *The Senses and Society*, 11 no.3 (2016): 251–61. www.doi.org/10.1080/17458927.2016.1195108.

pp. 104–105
Haptic Experience
Silvia Bombardini
Eco, Umberto. 'Lumbar Thought.' In *Fashion Theory: A Reader*, edited by Barnard Malcolm. London: Routledge, 2007.

Haraway, Donna J. *Simians, Cyborgs, and Women: The Reinvention of Nature*. New York: Routledge, 1991.

Negrin, Llewellyn. 'Maurice Merleau-Ponty: The Corporeal Experience of Fashion.' In *Thinking Through Fashion: A Guide to Key Theorists*, edited by Agnès Rocamora and Anneke Smelik, 115–31. London, New York: I.B. Tauris, 2016.

Young, Iris Marion. *On Female Body Experience: 'Throwing like a Girl' and Other Essays*. New York: Oxford University Press, 2005.

Working Together

pp. 114–115
Upside Down Dressing
Seohee Kim

pp. 116–117
The Intertextuality of Collab-oration
Laura & Deanna Fanning
    Kristeva, Julia. *Desire in Language: A Semiotic Approach to Literature and Art*. New York: Columbia University Press, 1980.
    Barthes, Roland. *Mythologies*. Translated by Annette Lavers. London, Paladin: Vintage [1972] 2009.
    Cronberg, Anja Aronowsky. 'On Fashion and Magic.' *Vestoj Issue* 2: Paris (January 2011).

pp. 118–119
Body Objects
Soft Baroque

pp. 120–121
Fashion for Community
Udochi Nwogu

pp. 122–123
Garments as Correspondence
Lenn Cox

pp. 124–125
Wearable Togetherness
Johanna Tagada Hoffbeck

pp. 128–129
PORTAL
Elisa van Joolen

Reading and Writing

pp. 138–139
'You wouldn't have noticed if you hadn't been told'
Dal Chodha
    Smith, Zadie. *A Hovering Young Man, Intimations*. Penguin Books, 2020
    Perec, Georges. *Thoughts of Sorts*. Boston: Godine, 2009.
    Chodha, Dal. *SHOW NOTES*. London: Tenderbooks, 2020
    Syms, Martine. *STRAIT*. Paris: Études Books n. 23, 2021.

I always tell my students: 'A style is a means of insisting on something.' A line of Sontag's. Every semester I repeat it, and every year the meaning of this sentence extends and deepens in my mind, blooming and multiplying like a virus, until it covers not just literary aesthetics and the films of Leni Riefenstahl but bedrooms, gardens, make-up, spectacles, camera angles, dances, gaits, gestures, sexual positions, haircuts, iPhone covers, bathroom taps, fonts, drink orders, dogs and people, and so much more – but people above all. Then semester ends and I forget all about it for a while.

pp. 140–141
Conversation Garments
Kasia Zofia Gorniak

pp. 142–143
Long-term Interview
Nakako Hayashi
Ingold, Tim. *Anthropology: Why it Matters.* Hoboken, New Jersey: John Wiley & Sons, 2018.
Takahashi, Mizuki and Nakako Hayashi. *You Reach Out—Right Now—for Something: Questioning the Concept of Fashion.* Exhibition catalogue February 22–May 18, 2014. Ibaraki, Japan: Mito Arts Foundation, 2014.
Hayashi, Nakako. 'Here and There.' *Hyacinth Revolution Issue* 13 (August 2018).

pp. 144–145
Wearing Ourselves on our T-shirts
Sang Thai
Thai, Sang. '"All Tee, No Shade": a Manifesto for a Subtle Critical Practice Negotiating Queer, East Asian Masculinities through T-shirts.' *Critical Studies in Men's Fashion* 8, no. 1–2 (2021): 93–110. www.doi.org/10.1386/csmf_00034_1
Barry, Ben. 'How Fashion Education Prevents Inclusivity.' *Business of Fashion*, January 06, 2020. www.businessoffashion.com/opinions/workplace-talent/op-ed-how-fashion-education-prevents-inclusivity/

pp. 148–149
(Mis)translation Workshop
Shanzhai Lyric
Apter, Emily. *Against World Literature: On the Politics of Untranslatability.* New York: Verso, 2013.
Chul-Han, Byung. *Shanzhai: Deconstruction in Chinese.* Cambridge: MIT Press, 2011.
Glissant, Eduoard. *Poetics of Relation.* Ann Arbor: University of Michigan Press, 1997.
Janecek, Jonathan. *Zaum: The Transrational Poetry of Russian Futurism.* San Diego: San Diego University Press, 1996.
Stalling, Jonathan. *Yingelishi: Sinophonic English Poetry and Poetics.* Denver: Counterpath Press, 2011.

pp. 152–153
Arbitrary Dictionary
Gabriele Monti
Clark, Judith, and Adam Phillips. *The Concise Dictionary of Dress.* London: Violette Editions, 2010.
Vries, Femke de. *Dictionary Dressings: Re-Reading Clothing Definitions Towards Alternative Fashion Perspectives.* Eindhoven: Onomatopee, 2016.

pp. 154–155
Writing a Garment
Dinu Bodiciu
Barthes, Ronald. *The Fashion System.* London: Vintage, 2010.

pp. 156–157
Head Butt Toe
Lou Hubbard
Studio Orta. 'Identity + Refuge.' Workshop reference 0436, 1995. www.studio-orta.com/en/artwork/539/identity-refuge-tie-dress
Caffaro, Giulia. 'Transfashional: Post-Interdisciplinary Lexicon. Moves to Rimini.' Exhibition and Catalogue by Dobrila Denegri, City Museum of Rimini–Modern Hall, October, 27 2019–January, 6 2020.' *ZoneModa Journal* 9, no. 2 (2019): 209–217. www.sustainable-fashion.com/publications/transfashional-%E2%80%93-post%2Finter%2Fdisciplinary-lexicon
Museum of Modern Art. 'Louise Bourgeois, Body Parts.' New York. www.moma.org/s/lb/curated_lb/themes/body_parts.html

pp. 158–159
Lexical Fashion Design
Liam Revell
Forty, Adrian. 'Language and Drawing.' In *Words and Buildings: a Vocabulary of Modern Architecture*, 29–41. London: Thames & Hudson, 2004.
Goldsmith, Kenneth. 'Language as Material.' In *Uncreative Writing: Managing Language in the Digital Age*, 34–62. New York: Columbia University Press, 2011.
Lehmann, Ulrich. 'Fashion as Translation.' *Art in Translation* 7, no. 2 (2015): 165–74.

pp. 162–163
Text as Material
Ruby Hoette
Goldsmith, Kenneth. *Uncreative Writing: Managing Language in the Digital Age.* New York: Columbia University Press, 2011.
Hoette, Ruby. 'Notes on Fashion Practice as Research: Episodes of Conversation Pieces.' In *Fashion Knowledge: Theories, Methods, Practices, and Politics*, edited by Elke Gaugele and Monica Titton, Bristol: Intellect, 2022.

Making, Finding, Tracing

pp. 170–171
The Dice Game
Anne Karine Thorbjørnsen

pp. 178–179
The Circle as Garment Form
Ashish Dhaka & Sonika Soni Khar

pp. 172–173
Abstract Form Making
Andrea Eckersley
    Almond, Kevin and Steve Swindells. 'Reflections on Sculptural Thinking in Fashion.' *Fashion Practice* 8, no.1 (2016): 44–62.

pp. 174–175
Abstract Patternmaking
Claudia Arana
    Rissanen, Timo and Holly McQuillan. *Zero Waste Fashion Design*. London: Bloomsbury Publishing, 2020.
    Lo, Dennic Chunman. *Pattern Cutting*. London: Laurence King Publishing, 2011. Accessed December 10, 2021. ProQuest Ebook Central.
    Nakamichi, Tomoko. *Pattern Magic* series. London: Laurence King Publishing, 2010.

pp. 176–177
Shadowear
Dinu Bodiciu
    Bodiciu, Dinu C.T. 'Shadowear: A New Way of Re(a)-dressing the Body.' In *Embodied Performativity in Southeast Asia, Multiple Corporealities* edited by Stephanie Burridge, 63–76. Oxton: Routledge, 2020.

pp. 180–181
Deletion Dressing
Remie Cibis
    Beckers, Anouk. *'JOIN Collective Clothes manual.'* Open-source modular garments system, 2019. www.joincollectiveclothes.com/manual
    Korporaal, Astrid. 'Censored Dresses.' *I Love You,* July 27, 2012: 14-19.
    Walther, Franz Erhard and Luis Croquer. *Franz Erhard Walther: The Body Draws*. Seattle: University of Washington, 2016.
    Van Joolen, Elisa and Ruby Hoette. ed. *11'x17' Reader*. Eindhoven: Onomatopee, 2014.
    Sampson, Ellen. *Worn: Footwear, Attachment and the Affects of Wear*, New York: Bloomsbury Publishing, 2020.
    Elfvik, Emilia. 'Cut and Paste: Exploring Two-Dimensional Material Collages for the Use in Clothing.' Bachelor Dissertation. University of Borås, 2015.

pp. 182–183
Blind Draping
Lidya Chrisfens
    Loar, Brian. 'Phenomenal States.' *Philosophical Perspectives* 4 (1990): 81–108. www.doi.org/10.2307/2214188
    Varela, Francisco J., Evan Thompson, and Eleanor Rosch. *The Embodied Mind: Cognitive Science and Human Experience*. London, England: MIT Press, 1993.
    Schmitz, Hermann, Rudolf Owen Müllan, and Jan Slaby. 'Emotions Outside the Box—the New Phenomenology of Feeling and Corporeality.' *Phenomenology and the Cognitive Sciences* 10, no. 2 (2011): 241–259. www.doi.org/10.1007/s11097-011-9195-1.

pp. 184–185
Designing with the Body
Patricia Wu Wu
    Geczy, Adam. *The Artificial Body in Fashion and Art: Marionettes, Models and Mannequins*. London: Bloomsbury Publishing, 2016.
    Wu, Patricia Wu. 'Practicing Fashion with the Anthropocene.' *Temes de Disseny* 35 (2019): 90–115.

pp. 186–187
Fade to Clay
Stéphanie Baechler

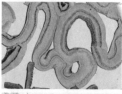

Re-viewing Images

pp. 196–197
Re-enacting the Fashion Image
Chet Julius Bugter
  Sobchack, Vivian. 'What My Fingers Knew: The Cinesthetic Subject, or Vision in the Flesh.' In *Carnal Thoughts: Embodiment and Moving Image Culture*, 53–84. Berkeley and Los Angeles: University of California Press, 2004.
  Shinkle, Eugenie. 'Uneasy Bodies: Affect, Embodied Perception and Contemporary Fashion Photography.' In *Carnal Aesthetics: Transgressive Imagery and Feminist Politics* edited by Marta Zarzycka and Bettina Papenburg 73–88. London and New York: I.B. Tauris, 2013.
  Best, Kate Nelson. *The History of Fashion Journalism*. London: Bloomsbury, 2017.
  Arngaard, Line and Sonia Oet. 'A March Issue.' Graduation Collaboration project. Rietveld Academie, 2018.

pp. 198–199
Bootleg Magazine
Federico Antonini &
Saul Marcadent
  Aletti, Vince. *Issues: A History of Photography in Fashion Magazines*. London–New York: Phaidon, 2019.
  Antonini, Federico. *Simplifying My Library: Episodes of Backward Shelving*. Zurich: everyedition, 2021.
  Lomme, Freek. *Can You Feel It? Effectuating Tactility and Print in the Contemporary*. Eindhoven: Onomatopee, 2018.
  Marcadent, Saul. *Publishing as Curating: Design and Imagery in Contemporary Fashion Magazines*. Venezia: Marsilio, 2020.
  Thoburn, Nicholas. *Anti-Book: On the Art and Politics of Radical Publishing*. Minneapolis: University of Minnesota Press, 2016.

pp. 200–201
Replica Relay Race
Shanna Soh

pp.202–203
Ways of Seeing (an Object)
Kate Meakin
  Berger, John. *Ways of Seeing: Based on the BBC Television Series with John Berger*. London: British Broadcasting Corporation, 1972.

pp. 206–207
Garment Photo Filter
Eleonora De Chiara

pp. 210–211
Fashion Image Questionnaire
Beata Wilczek
  Steyerl, Hito. 'In Defense of the Poor Image.' *e-flux journal*, no. 10 (November 2009). www.e-flux.com/journal/10/61362/in-defense-of-the-poor-image/

pp. 216–217
Chance, Systems, and Design Constraints
Jessie Kiely

Digging Deep

pp. 232–233
The Moral Economy of Fashion
Aurélie Van de Peer
Van de Peer, Aurélie and Lefevere, Merel. 'Little Doubts Everywhere.' *Vestoj Issue* 10 (2021): 159–169.
Sandel, Michael. *What Money Can't Buy: The Moral Limits of Markets*. New York: Farrar, Strauss & Giroux, 2012.
Widdows, Heather. *Perfect Me: Beauty as an Ethical Ideal*. Princeton, NJ: Princeton University Press, 2018.
McRobbie, Angela. 'Notes on the Perfect: Competitive Femininity in Neoliberal Times.' *Australian Feminist Studies* 30 (83): 3–20, 2015.
Bernard, Gert and Joshua Gert. 'The Definition of Morality.' In *Stanford Encyclopedia of Philosophy* (Fall 2020 Edition), edited by Edward N. Zalta. Stanford, CA: Stanford University, 2020. www.plato.stanford.edu/entries/morality-definition/.

pp. 234–235
Objects in Trouble: Rethinking Fashion Museum Collections
Marco Pecorari
Bal, Mieke. 'The Discourse of the Museum.' In *Thinking About Museums*, edited by Reesa Greenberg, Bruce Ferguson, and Sandy Nairne, 201–18. London, New York: Routledge, 1996.
Warhol, Andy. *Raid the Icebox*. April 23–June 30, 1970, RISD Museum, Providence, RI. www.risdmuseum.org/exhibitions-events/exhibitions/raid-icebox-1-andy-warhol
Karp, Ivan and Steven D. Lavine (eds.). *Exhibiting Cultures: The Poetics and Politic of Museum Display*. Washington and London: Smithsonian Institution Press, 1991.

pp. 236–237
Exercises on a Study Collection
Gabriele Monti
Martin, Richard. *Wordrobe*. New York: The Metropolitan Museum of Art, 1997.
Debo, Kaat, and Bob Verhelst. 'Patronen = Patterns.' Antwerp, Gent: Ludion, 2003.
i Ros, Rosa M. Martin, Pascale Gorguet-Ballesteros, Olivier Saillard, Alexandra Bosc, Marie-Laure Gutton, and Alexandre Samson. 'Cristobal Balenciaga: Collectionneur de Modes.' Paris: Paris-Musées, 2012.

pp. 238–239
The Social Life of Fashion Objects
Nicole K. Rivas
Chidlow, Kate, Sarah Pointon, and Lindie Ward. *Australian Dress Register: A User's Guide to the Care, Documentation, Interpretation and Display of Dress*. Powerhouse Museum, 2012. www.australiandressregister.org/media/pdf/resources/The_australian_dress_register_users_guide_august_2014_hires.pdf.
Vintage Fashion Guild. (n.d.). 'Label Resource: Guide to Vintage Labels.' Accessed January 16, 2019, www.vintagefashionguild.org/label-resource.

pp. 240–241
Look at Your Labels
Anika Kozlowski

pp. 242–243
Embodied Material Processes
Alice Lewis
Hutton, Jane. *Reciprocal Landscapes: Stories of Material Movements*. London and New York: Routledge, 2019.

pp. 244–245
Wardrobe Transparency
Harriette Richards
Egels-Zandén, Niklas, Kajsa Hulthén, and Gabriella Wulff. 'Trade-offs in Supply Chain Transparency: The Case of Nudie Jeans Co.' *Journal of Cleaner Production* 107 (2015): 95–104. www.doi.org/10.1016/j. jclepro.2014.04.074
James, Alana M., and Bruce Montgomery. 'Engaging the Fashion Consumer in a Transparent Business Model.' *International Journal of Fashion Design, Technology and Education* 10, no. 3 (2017.): 287–299. www.doi.org/10.1080/17543266.2017.1378730
Pham, Minh-Ha. T. 'The High Cost of High Fashion.' *Jacobin*, June 13, 2017. www.jacobinmag.com/2017/06/fast-fashion-labor-prada-gucci-abuse-designer
Richards, Harriette. 'Rethinking Value: "Radical Transparency" in Fashion.' *Continuum: Journal of Media and Cultural Studies*, (2021): 1–16. www.doi.org/10.1080/10304312.2021.1993575.

pp. 246–247
Unpicking Garments and Systems
Ruby Hoette
Iterations of the described method also appeared in:
Fletcher, Kate, and Ingun Grimstad Klepp. *Opening Up The Wardrobe*. Oslo: Novus Press, 2017.
Hoette, Ruby. 'Workshop—Unpicking the Fashion System.' In *Nordes 2015: Design Ecologies* at Konstfack–University College of Arts, Crafts and Design. Stockholm, Sweden, 7–10 June, 2015.

Sourcing and Re-sourcing

pp.258–259
Make your Own Modular Garments
Anouk Beckers
  Bruggeman, Daniëlle. *Dissolving the Ego of Fashion.* Arnhem: ArtEZ Press, 2018.
  Lauwaert, Maaike and Francien van Westrenen. *Facing Value.* Amsterdam: Valiz, 2016.
  Beckers, Anouk. 'JOIN Collective Clothes.' Open-source modular garments system, 2019. www.joincollective-clothes.com

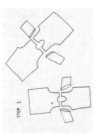

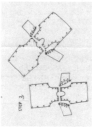

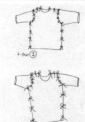

pp. 260–261
Re-making
Claire Myers

pp. 262–263
Meaningful Deconstruction
Anabel Poh
  Ingold, Tim. *Making: Anthropology, Archaeology, Art and Architecture.* London: Routledge, 2013.

pp. 264–265
Ideational Stocktake
Georgia McCorkill
  Adams, Erin. 'The Elements and Principles of Design: a Baseline Study.' *International Journal of Art & Design Education* 32, no. 2 (2013): 157–175.
  Eike, Rachel, Erin Irick, Ellen McKinney, Ling Zhang, and Eulanda Sanders. 'Repurposing Design Process.' In *Sustainability in the Textile and Apparel Industries,* edited by Subramanian Senthilkannan Muthu and Miguel Angel Gardetti, 189–239. Cham: Springer, 2020. www.doi.org/10.1007/978-3-030-37929-2_9
  McCorkill, Georgia. 'Triangles in Silk: Piecing Together a Practice of Upcycling.' Paper presented at the Shapeshifting, Auckland University of Technology April 14–16, 2014. www.openrepository.aut.ac.nz/handle/10292/8559.
  Schön, Donald A. *The Reflective Practitioner: How Professionals Think in Action.* New York: Basic Books, 1983.

pp. 266–267
Debris Assemblage
Rachael Cassar
  Hodder, Ian. *Entangled: An Archaeology of the Relationships Between Humans and Things.* New Jersey: Wiley Blackwell, 2012.
  Pels, Dick, Kevin Hetherington, and Frédéric Vandenberghe. 'The Status of the Object.' *Theory, Culture & Society* 19, no. 5-6 (2002): 1–21.
  Toadvine, Ted. *Merleau-Ponty's Philosophy of Nature.* Evanston, Illinois: Northwestern University Press, 2009.
  Kopytoff, Igor. 'The Cultural Biography of Things: Commoditization as Process.' *The Social Life of Things: Commodities in Cultural Perspective* 68 (1986): 70–73.

pp. 268–269
Wearing Your Waste
Johanna Tagada Hoffbeck
  Hoffbeck, Johanna Tagada. 'Penser, Manger, Partager.' www.johannatagada.net/Penser-Manger-Partager

pp. 270–271
Nearby Infinities
Maria Kley
Queneau, Raymond. *Exercises in Style*. London: Alma Books, 2018.

pp. 272–273
Temporary Loss
Clemens Thornquist
Seneca, Lucius Annaeus. *Moral Letters to Lucilius*. Vol. 3. Toronto: Aegitas, 2015.
Seneca, Lucius Annaeus. *Letters from a Stoic: Epistulae Morales ad Lucilium*. Vol. 210. London: Penguin UK, 1969.

Aïcha Abbadi (b. 1993) is an artist-designer and independent researcher. She studied at University of the Arts Berlin, explores niche fashion practices through collaborative projects, and works with local community spaces. Recent projects include: 'Gegenwarts-Werkstatt Mode' [Fashion Workshop of the Present]; Haus der Kulturen der Welt Berlin (HKW) [House of World Cultures] Schools of Sustainability in Berlin (2021/2022, with J. Schwab). Recent publications include: 'Trade Journals: From Performance Review to Runway Poetry' in *A Review of Reviews*, ed. H. van der Voet and J. Reponen (2021).

Abbadi lives and works in Berlin, Germany.
www.aichaabbadi.com

Federico Antonini (b. 1985) is a designer and artist. His investigation centres on the relationship between conceptual art and book-making and the (media) specificities of (re)production means. He has recently been featured in 'Retrofuturo,' MACRO, Museum of Contemporary Art of Rome (Rome, 2021). He is the author of *Simplifying my Library* (Everyedition, 2021); *Raising Moths* (NERO, 2019).
www.federicoantonini.info

Claudia Arana is an artist and fashion designer who studied at the National University of Colombia and Bunka Fashion Graduate University. She currently works in the Master's Degree program of Global Fashion Concentration (GFC) at Bunka Gakuen University, Tokyo. Her research focuses on sustainability and garment construction techniques such as whole garment machines, zero waste patternmaking, and upcycling. Recent publications include: 'Rediscovering Japanese Hemp Culture as a Design Practice for Sustainable Fashion,' *Journal of Bunka Gakuen University and Bunka Gakuen Junior College* 52 (2021).

Arana lives and works in Tokyo, Japan.
www.aranacl.com

Anja Aronowsky Cronberg (b. 1978) is a writer, researcher, and the founder of Vestoj—a think tank dedicated to why we wear what we wear. She studied fine art at Central Saint Martins (CSM) and history of design at the Royal College of Art/Victoria and Albert Museum (V&A) before founding Vestoj in 2009.

Vestoj was patroned by University of the Arts London (UAL) between 2013–2021, where Cronberg was also a senior research fellow in Fashion Theory and Practice. She has exhibited widely, including Palais de Tokyo; Lafayette Anticipations in Paris; and MoMA PS1 in New York. She is currently writing a book under contract with One World at Penguin Random House US.

Stéphanie Baechler (b. 1983) is an artist. She studied Textile Design at Lucerne University of Applied Sciences and Arts (HSLU) and completed a Master's in fashion at ArtEZ, Arnhem (NL). Stéphanie worked as a Textile Developer/Design Assistant for Hussein Chalayan in London and was Head of Print Design for the Swiss textile company Jakob Schlaepfer for three years. Her practice is situated at the intersection of textile and ceramics. Her research centres on the tactile dimension and the interaction between body, movement, and space.

She participated in shows and exhibitions at Chamber Gallery New York, Kunsthalle Fri Art Fribourg, The White House Gallery Belgium, PLUS-ONE Gallery Antwerp, Kunsthaus Centre d'art Pasquart Biel (CH), ISO Amsterdam (NL), and Mode Museum Antwerp (BE). Baechler attended several artists-in-residency programs in institutions such as the EKWC (European Ceramic Work Centre, NL) and Cité Internationale des Arts.

Stéphanie lives and works in Amsterdam and Switzerland.
www.stephaniebaechler.com

Linnea Bågander (b. 1986) is a senior lecturer of Artistic Research and Fashion Design at the Swedish School of Textiles. Through collaborations within the field of dance, she explores movement as design material, working with how material interprets and expresses the body's movements to how materials give impressions, inspiration and movements to the body and how this enables new bodies entwined with materials.

Recent exhibitions include: 'STM_16:9ftt,' exhibited in Critical Costume (Oslo, 2020), 'Fashion Clash' (Maastricht, NL, 2020); 'Transfashional' (City Museum of Rimini, IT, 2019). Recent performances include: 'Call of the Void,' (choreography

Nicole Neidert), Dansens Hus, (Stockholm, 2022). Recent publications include 'Body Movement as Material: Designing Temporal Expressions,' Doctoral Thesis (2021).

Bågander lives and works in Gothenburg (SE).
www.linneabagander.se

Laura Banfield (b. 1990) is an artist and an educator at RMIT University, Melbourne. Her work, spanning wearable artifacts, performance, installation, photography, and film, explores relationships between material, bodies, and fashion. Recent projects include: 'Performance of Postures, a Unique Fashion Performance' presented at NGV's Melbourne Design Week (2022); wearable artifact design for Confidence Man's international tour (2022); creative direction, photography, and installation design for Lambert's debut womenswear collection L1/22 (2021); and costume design for choreographer Deanne Butterworth's performance 'Slow Calm Drama' (2021).

Banfield lives and works in Naarm (Melbourne, AU).

Anouk Beckers (b. 1990) works as a designer and researcher. Beckers studied Textiles and Fashion at Gerrit Rietveld Academie (NL) and Social Psychology at Utrecht University (NL). Her practice creates a context in which to explore the field of fashion collaboratively, challenging some of fashion's core values, such as ownership, identity, originality, and authenticity. Beckers initiated an open-source modular clothing system 'Collective Clothes' (2019) and a series of wearable fashion magazines *Booklook* (2022). Recent workshops and exhibitions include: 'State of Fashion,' (NL, 2022); MAD (Brussels, BE, 2021); Textielmuseum (NL, 2021); Design Society Shenzhen (CN, 2021); RMIT (AU, 2020); Dutch Design Week (NL, 2020).

Beckers lives and works in Amsterdam (NL).
www.anoukbeckers.nl,
www.joincollectiveclothes.com,
www.booklook.website

Mary-Lou Berkulin (b. 1981) is a researcher and picture editor who studied Fashion Design at ArtEZ/the University of the Arts in Arnhem (NL). In 2018, she founded *Monument*, an independent fashion fanzine focusing on the (mostly analogue) archives of the Dutch Wave, a group of designers hailing from the nineties. Berkulin started her professional career as a designer and eventually started working as a fashion stylist. The (appearance of the) (fashion) image represents a constant fascination. Recent publications include: 'Oscar Suleyman,' *Monument* 3 (2021); 'Keupr/van Bentm,' *Monument* 2 (2020); 'Rozema/Teunissen,' *Monument* 1 (2018).

Berkulin lives and works in Amsterdam (NL).
www.monumentmagazine.nl

heeten bhagat (b. 1969) works in the emerging terrain of pracademics, expanding collaborations and design experiments between academia and real-life systems. His endeavours bring pragmatic and provocative programming to support decolonial and diversity-expanding processes in overlooked and underserved environments. His doctoral research/PhD 'Speculative Indigeneities— A [K]New Now' was accepted into the academy in 2019. One of his recent exhibitions was 'Re-Imagining The (Jagger) Library,' (Cape Town, ZA, 2022).

Dinu Bodiciu (b. 1979) is a designer-educator who studied at London College of Fashion and is currently a senior lecturer in Fashion at Leeds Beckett University. Dinu's research revolves around the interaction between the body and the dress approached as symbionts, interrogating the distribution of agency in the dressed body. His innovative approach to fashion includes Shadowear, a design method that negates the tridimensionality of the body and implicitly any traces of race, gender, and size to free the creative process.

Recent exhibitions include: 'On Display,' Vector 2.0 dance festival with dancer Lee Mun Wai (Esplanade, Singapore, 2022); 'Coucou Bazar,' group exhibition at Institute of Contemporary Arts (Singapore, 2022); 'Incantatio Mundi,' group exhibition at the Romanian Creative Week, (Iasi, Romania, 2022). Recent publications include: 'Shadowear: A New Way of Re(a)dressing the Body,' in *Embodied Performativity in Southeast Asia: Multidisciplinary Corporealities*, ed. Stephanie Burridge (Routledge, 2020).
www.dinubodiciu.com

Silvia Bombardini is a writer, researcher, lecturer, and film curator. She teaches at the London College of Communication and the Royal College of Art. Bombardini is a PhD candidate at Goldsmiths University, where her research on shoplifting as a feminist practice is part of the 'Politics of Patents (POP): Re-imagining Citizenship via Clothing Inventions 1820–2020' research project. Bombardini's interests include all forms of subversions in consumers' behaviour, and she has recently written a revaluation of counterfeits from postmodern and postcolonial perspectives. She used to run a 'Coming of Age' column for *Modern Weekly China*, on how global fashion trends reflect cultural and political shifts.
www.slvbmb.com

Chet Julius Bugter (b. 1994) is an artistic and embodied researcher, writer, and educator. He utters a cry of resistance against the neo-liberal, industrial fashion system, which denies the power and importance of the body at its centre. He works as head of programme of MA Critical Fashion Practices at ArtEZ University of the Arts (Arnhem, NL), and with fashion platform Warehouse. Recent publications include 'A Fruiting Body of Collective Labour' with Hanka van der Voet (ArtEZ Fashion Professorship, 2022); *Fat Belly Boy Booklet* (2020); and *Garments-Without-Bodies* (2019). He contributed to *Press & Fold* 02 (2022); *Press & Fold* 01 (2019); and *Tubelight* (2019).

Bugter lives and works in the Netherlands.
www.chetjulius.com

Otto von Busch (b. 1975) is a designer, and associate professor of Integrated Design at Parsons School of Design. In his work he explores how the powers of fashion can be bent to achieve a positive personal and social condition with which the Everyperson is free to grow to their full potential.

Von Busch lives and works in New York.
www.selfpassage.info

Francesca Capone (b. 1987) is a visual artist, writer, and materials designer. Her work is concerned with the creation of materials and a poetic consideration of their meaning. She is interested in how tactile forms simultaneously serve as

functional surfaces for daily life and as a mode of communication or symbol within the cultural paradigm. Her book *Weaving Language I: Lexicon* (Essay Press, 2022), is part of a multi-book series focused on textile poetics. Her books are in the collections of the MoMA Library and the Watson Library at the Metropolitan Museum of Art. She has been an artist in residence at the Josef and Anni Albers Foundation. She is represented by Nationale, Portland (US).
www.francescacapone.com

Rachael Cassar (b. 1984) is a designer and lecturer at the University of Technology Sydney. Her research is driven by a long-term engagement with sustainable fashion processes connected to her established fashion upcycling practice RACHAEL CASSAR. Rachael has worked within the industry for fifteen years, experimenting with deconstruction and reformation. Her current PhD explores the research and documentation processes inherent to working with historic archival information embedded within material artefacts. Recent publications include 'The Reading of the Piece: An Upcycler's Embodied Experience of Working with Material Culture of the Deceased,' *Fashion Practice* 13 no. 3 (2021): 331–350.
www.rachaelcassar.com

Dal Chodha (b. 1982) is a lecturer and writer. He is editor-in-chief of *Archivist Addendum*: a publishing project that explores the gap between fashion editorial and academia. Chodha leads the first year of the BA Fashion Communication & Promotion course at Central Saint Martins, London, whilst a regular contributor to titles including *i-D*, *Modern Matter*, and *Wallpaper**. In 2020 he self-published *SHOW NOTES*— an original hybrid of journalism, poetry, and provocation.

Chodha lives and works in London.
www.dalchodha.com

Lidya Chrisfens (b. 1985) is a practice-based fashion practitioner, researcher, and educator at Lasalle College of the Arts, Singapore. Her research focuses on new methodologies exploring interdisciplinary approaches in new phenomenology such as Atmospheric Space and Conceptual Space to

express her conceptual development thoughts into ideas. Her work explores the relationship between the designer's bodily experience, memories, emotion, and clothing in the process of making. She has presented her recent research at various design conferences, such as 'Design Principle & Practices' (2021, 2023) and the International Foundation of Fashion Technology Institutes (2021, 2022).
www.lidyachrisfens.com

Remie Cibis is a critical fashion practitioner and lecturer in Fashion & Textiles at RMIT University, Melbourne. Her work explores how fashion images are produced and seeks to design opportunities for wearers to fashion their own representations through the use of garment-making, image-making, workshops, critical theory, and deconstructivist design practices. Recent projects include: 'Ready-to-Wear,' KINGS Artist Run (Melbourne, 2022); 'Less is More, More or Less,' Sarah Scout Presents (Melbourne, 2020); and 'The Fashion Edit,' University of Auckland (Auckland, 2019).
www.remiecibis.com

Marieke Coppens (b. 1980) is a visual artist, social psychologist, researcher, tutor, guru, writer, and ghost-writer for her cats. She studied at OTIS College of Art and Design (Los Angeles) and Sandberg Instituut (Amsterdam). She is currently collaborating with buildings, materials—like clothes—and (non-)human animals. In 2020 she collaborated with Art Chapel Amsterdam performing a chalk ritual. She is also present at art fairs like This Art Fair (NL, 2022), OBJECT Rotterdam (NL, 2022) and BIG ART (Amsterdam, 2021) and had solos at Posthoornkerk Amsterdam (2019) and SCHUNCK Heerlen (NL, 2018).
Coppens lives and works in Amsterdam.
www.mariekecoppens.be,
www.healingheptagon.com

Lenn Cox (b. 1985) is a community organizer, designer, educator, curator, and karateka. Cox graduated in 2020 from the ArtEZ MA Practice Held in Common (Arnhem, NL), initiating and co-creating the manual *Collective Wandering: Hanging Out with Our Everyday Ecology.* Cox explores self-organized learning-working-living environments while ritualizing her clothing as a logbook. Fashion, for Cox, is an embodied and relational practice rooted in everyday life. In 2019 she initiated z o m e r k a m p collective to explore what it means to have a collective practice at this time.
Cox lives in Arnhem (NL), and works wandering.

Eleonora De Chiara is an art director and stylist. She holds a BA in Communication Design at University of Architecture in Naples (IT). Upon completing her studies, she continued her personal research focusing mainly on fashion communication materials. She is currently the art director and stylist of Paloma Wool's image department. Her work focuses on the creation and production of images through fabrics and photography. She is interested in the relationship between personal memories and clothes.
www.palomawool.com

Ashish Dhaka is an academic, entrepreneur, and researcher working on creative explorations that originate from the traditional art and craft of India, encompassing the tangible and intangible heritage. 'I belong to a country which has a rich textile heritage that has gone through countless changes in the past decades. The only thing that has remained constant in this evolution is the need to 'dress.' This very need becomes the cornerstone of my existence as a fashion designer and educator.'
Ashish is collaborating with Sonika S. Khar on their ongoing practice on ply-split braiding and utilizes post-consumer and post-production textile waste to create modular garments and accessories. Sustainability for them means accessing each stage of the supply chain and developing methodologies inspired from Indian culture to mitigate waste and negative impact on the planet. They have represented India as finalists at 'World of Wearable Art' 2019 and 2020, Wellington (NZ).

Paola Di Trocchio (b. 1981) is a fashion curator, and writer. She is currently the programme manager at PayPal Melbourne Fashion Festival. From 2002 to 2022, she was a curator in the fashion and textiles department at the National Gallery of Victoria, curating and co-curating twenty-two exhibitions with accompanying publications. Paola completed her MA (Fashion) at RMIT University, Melbourne and is currently completing her doctorate at Queensland University of Technology (QUT), Brisbane. Her research explores the application of curatorial principles outside the museum setting and focuses on a close study of fashion journalist and style maverick Anna Piaggi.

Andrea Eckersley (b. 1976) is an artist and senior lecturer in the School of Fashion and Textiles at RMIT University, Melbourne. Primarily interested in the way the body interacts with abstract shapes, Eckersley's work treats surfaces, affects, and materials as central to the realization and experience of an artwork. Recently co-authored publications include 'Bodies of Fashion and the Fashioning of Subjectivity,' *Body and Society* (2020) and *Practicing with Deleuze: Design, Dance, Art, Writing, Philosophy* (Edinburgh University Press, 2017). Andrea is the art editor *Deleuze and Guattari Studies* and exhibits regularly in Australia.
www.andreaeckersley.com

Aimilia Efthimiou (b. 1994) is an artist. She studied fine arts in the Athens School of Fine Art and at the Piet Zwart Institute in Rotterdam. Her practice is an enchanting exploration of magic as a remedy and weapon against patriarchal structures. Recent exhibitions include: 'Summer love tarot readings,' Recyclart (Brussels, 2022); 'w139 hosts....,' performance event, W139 (Amsterdam, 2022); KVTV television episode 2, performance event organized by the KVTV collective (Frankfurt 2021); 'Sunday the day of the sun,' organized by From Brussels to EU with love, Recyclart (Brussels, 2021); 'Material Contexts,' Het Archief (Rotterdam, 2021). Recent publications include: 'Plant Magic Poison & Remedy,' hoops collective (2022); 'FDBNHLLLTTFNOCTURNAL' *stickyfingers publishing* (Winter 2021); 'Soul Death in a Digital Dating App 2021,' *Coven Berlin*; 'Magic and Spiritual Rituals' *Kunstlicht*, Spellbound (2021); *DAISYWORLD MAGAZINE*, no. 2 (2021).
Efthymiou lives and works in Rotterdam.
www.aimiliaefthimiou.com

Laura and Deanna Fanning (b. 1990) live and work in London (UK). For the past six years they have collaborated on fashion-led projects. Currently they creatively direct the womenswear collections and collaborations at Kiko Kostadinov. Laura holds a B.DES (Fashion) from RMIT University, Melbourne, and an MA Fashion (Womenswear) from CSM/ Central Saint Martins University, London. Deanna holds a BA (International Relations) from La Trobe University, Melbourne and a BA and MA Fashion (Knitwear) from CSM/Central Saint Martins University.

Chinouk Filique de Miranda (b. 1991) works as a Design Researcher and Critical (Fashion) Practitioner. In her work she analyzes, translates, and visualizes the crossover between the fashion system and digital culture with a focus on introducing digital literacy into fashion. In addition to her independent practice, she (co-) designs workshops for educational programmes and lectures on (digital) fashion, design, and consumer engagement at various cultural institutions. She was the Guest-Editor of *Fashion Studies Journal*'s first ever Specials' issue, which focused on Fashion & Digital Engagement (2022). She has collaborated with institutions such as Warehouse, Cooper Hewitt, Het Nieuwe Instituut, National Museum of African American History and Culture, State of Fashion, and Onomatopee. She holds an MA in Critical Fashion Practices from ArtEZ, Arnhem (2019, NL) and a BA in Lifestyle Transformation Design from the Willem de Kooning Academy, Rotterdam (2013, NL).

She is currently located between Rotterdam, Amsterdam, and the online realm.
www.chinoukfilique.info

Kate Fletcher is a professor at the Royal Danish Academy, Copenhagen. As an active scholar in the field of fashion and sustainability, she challenges and defines discourses on post-growth fashion, fashion localism, decentring durability, and Earth Logic. She has written and/or edited ten books available in eight languages. She is a co-founder of the Union of Concerned Researchers in Fashion. Her latest work is about design and nature.
www.katefletcher.com

Laura Gardner (b. 1987) is an editor, lecturer, and co-publisher of *Mode and Mode*. She holds a PhD from RMIT University, Melbourne, and her research and projects focus on the methodologies of experimental fashion publishing in proximity to other creative fields. She is currently lecturing at the School of Fashion and Textiles at RMIT and is a freelance writer and editor. Formerly online editor for the journal *Vestoj*, she has written for *Monument*, *299 792 458 m/s*, *Press & Fold*, *Flash Art* Online, *Dirty Furniture* magazine and *BON*. Talks and panels include Printing Fashion, NGV Art Book Fair Symposium, RMIT Design Hub, and Lyonhousemuseum. She is a guest lecturer at ArtEZ, Arnhem (NL), and London College of Fashion (UAL).

Gardner lives and works in Melbourne (AU).
www.lauragardner.co

Abigail Glaum-Lathbury is an artist and designer based in Mexico City and Chicago. Her work explores the discursive potential found in clothing and dressing, arguing for a rethinking and transformation of the fashion system. Glaum-Lathbury's work has been shown at the MoMA and MAD Museum in New York and the MCA Chicago. Her projects have been covered in the *New York Times*, the *Paris Review*, and *The Guardian*, among others. She is an associate professor of Fashion Design at the School of the Art Institute of Chicago.
www.abigailglaumlathbury.com

Julie Gork is a fashion researcher and theorist who studied at Parsons School of Design and is currently completing her PhD at RMIT University, Melbourne. She currently works as a researcher at RMIT PlaceLab. Her research focuses on experiences of the dressed body, from everyday dress to fashioning the cyborg body. Her doctoral research complicates fashion's ocularcentrism through the stories and knowledges of people with vision impairments.

Julie lives and works in Naarm, Melbourne, on Wurundjeri Country in Australia.
www.juliegork.com

Kasia Zofia Gorniak (b. 1987) is a fashion designer based in Helsinki (FI), originally from Melbourne (AU). She completed a Master of Arts in Art & Design at Aalto University, Helsinki, and a Bachelor of Design (Fashion) at RMIT University, Melbourne. In 2018 Gorniak established her primary practice, called 'talking through our bodies'—a knitwear label with pieces formed through collaborative and performative design processes. Recently, she has been working on two research projects for Aalto University with a focus on innovations in sustainable textiles.
www.kasiagorniak.com

Nakako Hayashi (b. 1966) is a writer, editor, and curator. She is currently studying for a Master of Research degree in Exhibition Studies at Central Saint Martins, London. In dialogue with selected artists/designers (such as Susan Cianciolo and Bless) she has been facilitating the *Here and There Magazine* since 2002. An exhibition based on her book *Kakucho suru Fashion* [Expanded Fashion] (DU Books, 2011) was realized in 2014.

Recent group exhibitions include: 'Modus:Hosts' Fashion Square Gallery (London, Oct.–Dec. 2022). Supervising exhibitions: 'Photography and Fashion since the 1990s' Tokyo Photographic Art Museum (Tokyo, 2020); 'You Reach Out–Right Now–for Something: Questioning the Concept of Fashion' Contemporary Art Centre, Art Tower Mito, Mito and Marugame Genichiro Inokuma Museum of Contemporary Art (Marugame, 2014); 'Baby Generation' Parco Space Part 3 (Tokyo, 1996). Recent publications: *Tsukuru Riyuu* [Reasons to Create] (2021); *Kakucho suru Fashion* [Expanded Fashion] (2014).

Hayashi lives and works in Tokyo.

Marjanne van Helvert (b. 1982) is a designer, writer, and educator. She studied Textiles at the Rietveld Academie Amsterdam and Cultural Studies at the Radboud University Nijmegen. Projects include the 'Dirty Design Manifesto' (2013); *The Responsible Object: A History of Design Ideology for the Future*, ed. (Valiz, 2016); and *A Library for Material Rights* (Stroom, 2018). She explores past, present, and future design ideologies, focusing especially on ecology, degrowth, and feminism.

Van Helvert lives in Amsterdam (NL).
www.dirty-design.net

Ruby Hoette (b. 1983) is a senior lecturer in Design at Goldsmiths, University of London. Her work as a designer and educator seeks to expand what constitutes fashion practice through critical and experimental modes of engaging with and producing fashion. Negotiating existing objects, processes, and infrastructures, and the traces of social, cultural, and economic interactions they carry, her work unpicks and reconfigures relationships between garment and system, theory and practice. She is co-founder of MODUS: a platform for expanded fashion practice with Caroline Stevenson.

Hoette lives and works in London and the Netherlands. www.rubyhoette.com

Lou Hubbard (b. 1957) is an artist and writer who teaches at the School of Art, Victorian College of the Arts, University of Melbourne. Hubbard uses strategies of DADA, Surrealism, and Arte Povera to understand the nature of training and submission in the behaviour of her body at work and play. Recent exhibitions include: 'It's dark. This is it. It's stuck,' Dungeon (Melbourne, 2021); 'Walkers with Dinosaurs,' MEJIA (Melbourne, 2021); 'Operative,' Sarah Scout Presents (Melbourne, 2020); 'The Léger Melee,' MOFO (Launceston, 2019). www.louhubbard.com

Marie Hugsted (b. 1977) is a textile designer who studied at the Royal Danish Academy. She works in the field between exploration and design. Hugsted is interested in textures, patterns, materials, colours, and surfaces connected to the textile field. She works with natural dyes, tufting, knit, and textile print always giving an emphasis on sustainability. Being both designer and teacher by profession, her core focus is to disseminate knowledge about design in various ways— as lecturer, designer, and writer.

Hugsted lives and works in Copenhagen, Denmark. www.hugsted.dk

Elisa van Joolen (b. 1983) is a designer and artist. She was a participant at Jan van Eyck Academy, Maastricht (2019/2020) and at IASPIS, Stockholm (2016), where she co-founded the Warehouse platform, 'A Place for Clothes in Context,' and lecturer at Gerrit

Rietveld Academie, Amsterdam. Van Joolen's projects expose relational aspects of clothing and subvert processes of value production. Recent exhibitions/projects include: 'It's Our F*** Backyard,' Stedelijk Museum (Amsterdam, 2022); 'Fitting in,' Z33 House for Contemporary Art, Design and Architecture, (Hasselt, BE, 2022); 'PORTAL 012,' Design Museum, Den Bosch ('s-Hertogenbosch, NL, 2022). Publications include *Our Rags Magazine* co-edited with Aimée Zito Lema (Warehouse, 2022).

Van Joolen lives and works in Amsterdam. www.elisavanjoolen.com

Sanne Karssenberg is a programme-maker, process designer, and educator. Her work has a strong focus on design as an interface for enhancing socio-political interactivity between the wearer, maker, participant, student, their surroundings, and more. She currently works as a programme maker at Bureau Ruimtekoers, Arnhem (NL); as a process designer at ELIA, European League of the Institutes of the Arts, Amsterdam; teaches at the Rietveld Academie Fashion Department, and works on a publication about her former work as project coordinator of Civic Praxis at BAK (basis voor actuele kunst) in Utrecht (NL). Karssenberg graduated from the Gerrit Rietveld Academie (BA) and from the Sandberg Insituut (MA), Amsterdam (NL). www.sannekarssenberg.nl

Noorin Khamisani is a fashion designer, researcher, and educator focused on fashion design for sustainability and circularity, informed by a decade of professional practice. Challenging the current fashion system is a key theme of Khamisani's teaching work, where students reimagine the future of fashion. Her current research explores decolonizing, digitization, and sustainability within fashion practice and education. She is a member of the Union of Concerned Researchers in Fashion. www.noorinkhamisani.com

Sonika Soni Khar (PhD) has been teaching Design, Craft Studies, and Innovation and Research and Research Methods to undergraduates, graduates, and master level students for the last seventeen years. Her PhD research focused on the gap between the design pro-

cess practiced in the industry and the manner in which it is being taught in fashion design institutes, deriving a teaching a method therein.

Her work focusses not only on theoretical research on design process/pedagogies but also on its application in product development (Fashion and Textiles) and in using craft and craft technique. She designed costumes for the Oscar-nominated film in the foreign-language category *Paheli* directed by Amol Palekar in 2005. Publications include *DHAROHAR: The Reflections of Indian Heritage* (Copal, Ghaziabad, IN, 2019). Projects include her garment entry 'Ganga: to earth from heaven,' selected as a finalist from India in the 'World of Wearable Art' (Wellington, NZ, 2018).

Jessie Kiely (b. 1989) is a Womenswear Designer and lecturer at RMIT University School of Fashion and Textiles, Melbourne. She has worked in France, London, and Melbourne. Kiely's work approach develops design systems and methodologies affecting research, construction, and art direction within collections. Recent exhibitions/projects include: 'Apparel,' Neon Park (Melbourne, 2021); 'SS22 Poetry and Motion,' Perks and Mini (Melbourne, 2021); 'Fall 2020 (Ready-to-Wear),' Isabel Marant (Paris, 2020). Recent publications include: 'Art for All' *Mode and Mode* 6 (2020).

Kiely lives and works in Melbourne (AU). www.jessiekiely.com

Seohee Kim (b. 1991) is a fashion designer and graduate of the Royal College of Art (London). She currently runs her project label SEHIKYO based in Seoul. In this studio project, all clothes represent a visual metaphor for the sophisticated experience of the wearer's emotions, movements, and the spaces surrounding them. SEHIKYO reflects on the personal and social meaning of 'wearing' while re-contextualizing clothing in a context far from the consumer culture. Selected projects include: 'Magic loop,' Gallery Philosophie (Seoul, 2022); 'The skirt,' MMCA Residency Changdong (Seoul, 2022); 'Wear Wore Worn,' The reference (Seoul, 2021); 'Ways of dressing,' (Seoul, 2019). www.sehikyo.org

Maria Kley (b. 1981) is a visual artist based in Brussels. She studied fashion design at ArtEZ University of the Arts in Arnhem (NL). From 2018–2019, she was a resident at the Rijksakademie van beeldende kunsten, Amsterdam.

Primarily a sculptor, Kley's hybrid practice includes sculptural portraits and architectural installations as well as drawing, video, and performance. Each artwork derives from a deep connection to intimate narratives, materials, and the passage of time. Each work is a physical manifestation of existential questioning, a process that goes hand in hand with extensive material research and is open to participation. www.mariakley.com

Anika Kozlowski (PhD) is an inter-disciplinary researcher, designer, and educator in sustainable fashion. Her work uses a system thinking framework while drawing on her background in microbiology, environmental science, and fashion design. She is interested in exploring the use of design and systems thinking in developing alternative hyper-local modes of responsible and regenerative clothing practices in managing fashion textile waste. Kozlowski is also an expert on the design and business practices of sustainably minded micro-and-small fashion enterprises (MSEs). With a research approach that is strongly practice-based, Kozlowski continues to directly work with MSEs in the transition to circular and regenerative fashion practices. www.anikakozlowski.com

Valerie Lange (b. 1976) is a fashion designer currently teaching at the Academy of Fine Arts Vienna and at the University of Arts Linz (AT). She has been working as a creative pattern maker for the Belgian fashion designer Christian Wijnants since 2005. With her former fashion label DIPTYCH, Lange repeatedly tried to act outside of common demands of the fashion industry. For example, in 2012 DIPTYCH presented a One-Piece-collection that featured one single jumpsuit on thirteen different bodies. With the introduction of ten key looks that were available over several seasons, DIPTYCH refused the demand for constant renewal. In her teaching, Lange focuses on methods and procedures for translating abstract informa-

tion (moods, atmospheres, attitudes, concepts etc.) into physical design pieces and on analyzing and decoding existing design objects.

Ulrik Martin Larsen (b. 1975) is an artist/designer/researcher currently working as a senior lecturer in Fashion Design at the Swedish School of Textiles (Borås, SE) and as one half of the interdisciplinary artist duo PUTPUT. In his research and artistic practice there is a focus on the relationship between object/body/image and on interactions with the objects we use, abuse, and admire in everyday life.

Exhibitions include: 'EXTRA NORMAL,' Bygning A (Copenhagen, 2022/23); 'Subversive Design,' NRW Forum (Düsseldorf, 2022); 'Cavities,' Tableau (Copenhagen, 2021); 'Jonald Dudd,' New York Design Week (2021); 'Drafts,' Art Triennial UFNA Unpredictable Future (Lithuania 2021).

Larsen lives and works in Copenhagen, Denmark and Borås (SE). www.ulrikmartinlarsen.com, www.putput.dk

Maaike Lauwaert (b. 1978) is a writer and the Chair of the Executive Board of the Gerrit Rietveld Academie, Amsterdam. She studied at the University of Maastricht (NL), was business director at de Appel Amsterdam (2016–2022), and worked at Stroom Den Haag (NL) and the Mondriaan Foundation (NL). She co-edited with Francien van Westrenen the volume *Facing Value: Radical Perspectives from the Arts* (Valiz, 2017). She has published on contemporary art in various magazines. www.maaikelauwaert.com

Alice Lewis (b. 1988) is lecturer and programme leader of the Master's of Landscape Architecture at RMIT University, Melbourne. She holds a PhD from the same institution. Her interdisciplinary design research practice explores the impact of human action as an active constituent of landscape systems, using prostheses and counter mapping to question anthropocentric perspectives and engage the generative force of human action as caregivers for environments. Recent publications focus on developing design pedagogies for responding to climate emergencies.

Matthew Linde is a fashion exhibition-maker, researcher, and writer. He holds a PhD from RMIT University, Melbourne (2021), where his practice-based research focused on the curatorial and communicative scope of fashion—specifically, the 'boutique' as an experimental and performative site. He previously ran Centre for Style, an exhibition space and store for contemporary fashion practice. Linde has also curated a number of fashion and art exhibitions at Gertrude Contemporary (AU), Mathew Gallery (US), the Goethe-Institut's Ludlow38 (US), Kunsthalle Bern (CH), and the Berlin Biennale.

Linde is currently based in New York. www.matthewlinde.com

Saul Marcadent (b. 1984) is a researcher at the Iuav University of Venice, where he leads the Publishing Atelier. His research activity focuses on the interaction between the approach to publishing and a theoretical and critical perspective. He is currently managing editor of *Dune*, a biannual academic journal published by *Flash Art*. He is the author of *Publishing as Curating: Design and Imagery in Contemporary Fashion Magazines* (Marsilio, 2020). www.about.me/saulmarcadent

Marco Marino is a designer and an independent researcher. He holds a BA in Fashion Design from Iuav University of Venice and works across product development, special projects, and creative strategies for companies, institutions, and studios. He is co-founder of Rotonda Studio and external collaborator with the Fashion Theory and History pathway at Iuav. His research focuses on the relationships between the circulation strategies of art and the fashion system, with a specific interest in the social role of retail spaces.

Marino lives and works in Venice. www.rotonda.studio

Georgia McCorkill is a lecturer at RMIT University, School of Fashion and Textiles, Melbourne. McCorkill's practice-based research explores sustainable garment-making strategies such as upcycling, repair, and co-design alongside alternative models of fashion consumption such as sharing. Recent projects include:

'Fashion.Craft.Repair' Craft Contemporary Festival (Melbourne 2020); 'Fashion Fix' Melbourne Fashion Festival (2020). Recent conference publications include 'Ideational Stocktake: Poetic Processes for Material Repurposing' (2021); 'Fashion Fix: Exploring Garment Repair from a Critical Fashion Practice Perspective' (2021).

McCorkill lives and works in Melbourne (AU).
www.georgiamccorkill.id.au

Kate Meakin is a visual artist based in Naarm/Melbourne (AU). She is currently undertaking a practice-based PhD with RMIT University's School of Fashion and Textiles, Melbourne. Her project examines the social dynamics of fashion image production through the 'Behind the scenes' film genre. Meakin often collaborates with other artists and fashion practitioners as a filmmaker and photographer. Recent exhibitions include 'The body speaks before it even talks,' 99% gallery (Melbourne, 2022); 'Fashion Moves,' ASVOFF 13 (Paris, 2021); 'On Time,' Connors Connors (Melbourne, 2020).
www.katemeakin.net

Daphne Mohajer va Pesaran is an Iranian-Canadian designer and academic. She is programme manager of the Bachelor of Textiles (Design) and lectures in Fashion and Textiles Design and research in The School of Fashion and Textiles at RMIT University in Melbourne (AU). She spent ten years living and working in Tokyo, where she learned about many traditional craft practices. She likes collaborating and is interested in what materials and relationships can emerge in communities of human and nonhuman people. In her research and design practice she works with handmade Japanese paper and garments/products made from paper, and recent research fellowships include the British Museum and the Australian Museum to research the use of paper for clothing in Japan and the Pacific Islands.
www.d-mvp.com

Gabriele Monti (b. 1978) (PhD) is associate professor at Iuav University of Venice, where he coordinates the BA programme in Fashion Design and Multimedia Arts. Among his research interests are theories of fashion design, visual culture, and fash-

ion curating. He is a member of the editorial board of *Dune* journal and of the scientific committee of the European Fashion Heritage Association (EFHA). Recent exhibitions and catalogues include: 'Italiana: Italy Through the Lens of Fashion 1971–2001,' Palazzo Reale (Milan, 2018); 'Bellissima: Italy and High Fashion 1945–1968,' MAXXI (Rome, 2014). Recent publications include: *In posa: Modelle italiane dagli anni cinquanta a oggi* [Posing: Italian Fashion Models from the Fifties Up to Now] (Marsilio, 2016).

Monti lives and works in Venice.

Claire Myers (b. 1994) is a fashion practitioner and founder of womenswear label Lambert and also works as a freelance pattern maker and machinist. Myers cut her teeth as a pattern maker in the atelier at Molly Goddard in London after graduating from the fashion design program at RMIT, Melbourne in 2018. Her body of work focuses on unconventional pattern-making methods, working within the limitations of existing materials and objects to draw out new garment and accessory propositions from those that have previously been produced and discarded. Recent exhibitions include: 'Performance of Postures' (co-produced with Laura Banfield), Royal Park (Melbourne, 2022); 'Lambert: Moving Parts,' Reina (Melbourne, 2022); 'Fort Earth' Group Show, Marfa Gallery (Melbourne, 2021).

Myers lives and works in Melbourne (AU).
www.lambertdress.com

Udochi Nwogu (b. 1983) is a business professional and entrepreneur. She studied for her undergraduate degree at Georgetown University School of Foreign Service (Washington DC) and at the Wharton School, University of Pennsylvania where she received her MBA. She currently serves as a consultant for start-ups in the technology sector and manages two organizations she co-founded focused on the African fashion sector-retail platform—It's Made To Order and the non-profit Building African Fashion (formerly Bias In African Fashion).

Sanem Odabaşı (b. 1989) is a scholar and artist. Her practices include sustainable fashion,

critical fashion, material culture, and practice-based research. She continues her academic life at Eskişehir Technical University, Department of Textile and Fashion Design (TR). She has been involved in many academic and artistic activities. Her first book *Sürdürülebilir Moda Tasarımı: Kavramlar ve Uygulamalar* [Sustainable Fashion Design: Concepts and Practices] was released in 2022.

Naoko Ogawa (b. 1979) is a jewellery artist. She studied at Tokyo University of the Arts. The focus of her practice questions what jewellery can be. Based on personal experience rather than contemporary values, she carefully studies what people find joyful and beautiful, and creates jewellery as a device to experience this elevation of the mind.

Recent exhibitions include: 'Reflection,' gallery deux poisons (Tokyo, 2022); 'PLAY JEWELLERY - wearing, making, thinking-,' Tokyo Metropolitan Teien Art Museum (Tokyo, 2015); 'Jewelry Hunting—Die Jagd nach dem Schmuckbild,' Schmuck2 HOCHsitz Atelier, (Retschow, DE, 2013). Recent publications include: *Jewelry Hunting—Book—* (2022).

Ogawa lives and works in Berlin.
naokoogawa.com,
www.jewelryhunting.com

Oluwasola Kehinde Olowo-Ake (b. 1998) is a designer, storyteller, and an independent researcher. She studied Fashion Design at Nottingham Trent University (UK) and a Master of Design at Emily Carr University, Vancouver (CA). Her design practice focuses on using Yorùbá storytelling methods to speak into issues regarding the black race that she encounters and additionally depict narratives that are befitting of black bodies—through dance, song, ways of wearing, and poetry. Recent exhibitions include: 'I see; I breathe; I am,' Surrey Art Gallery (Vancouver, 2022); 'UN-VEILING,' Slice of Life Gallery (Vancouver, 2022).

Olowo-Ake lives and works on the unceded territories of the səlilwətaʔɬ təməxw (Tsleil-Waututh), Skwxwú7mesh-ulh Temíx w (Squamish), Sʼólh Téméxw (Stó:lō), Stz'uminus and šxwməθkwəy̓əmaʔɬ təməxw (Musqueam) Nations.
www.kehindeolowoake.com

PAGEANT: Amanda Cumming & Kate Reynolds work as collaborators under the umbrella of PAGEANT, an independent fashion practice established by the pair in 2010. Drawing inspiration from diverse realms within art, music, and culture and praised for their innovation and ingenuity, PAGEANT collections advocate an alternate vision of femininity and masculinity that is fresh, fierce, and current. Their garments are forged from technically sophisticated fabrics, with aesthetic odes to sportswear.

Amanda and Kate live and work in Naarm/Melbourne on Wurundjeri Country (AU).
www.wearepageant.com

Marco Pecorari (PhD) is programme director of the MA in Fashion Studies at Parsons Paris where he teaches and conducts research on Fashion History and Theory. His recent research focuses on the politics of archives and museums, exploring the intersections between critical theory, fashion media, performance, and heritage. He is the author of *Fashion Remains: Rethinking Fashion Ephemera in the Archive* (Bloomsbury, 2021) and co-editor of *Fashion, Performance and Performativity: The Complex Spaces of Fashion* (Bloomsbury, 2021).

Anabel Poh (b. 1998) is a Singaporean textile designer who studied at Design Academy Eindhoven (NL), co-founder of UNCOLOUR, and Luxury & Material innovations team lead. Her works often have a strong emotional resonance with people, objects, and the world around them, exploring ideas of emotional durability and preservation of crafts. Recent exhibitions include: 'Fashion as Encounters,' State of Fashion Biennale, EusebiusKerk, (Arnhem, NL, 2022); 'Gent Design Fest,' Design Museum Gent (Ghent, BE, 2022); 'Graduation 2021, Dutch Design Week,' Beursgebouw (Eindhoven, NL, 2021); '1m2,' Dutch Design Week, Van Abbemuseum (Eindhoven, NL, 2021).

Poh lives and works in Eindhoven (NL).
www.anabelpoh.studio

PUGMENT is a Tokyo-based fashion label founded in 2014. We observe the process by which the value and meaning of clothing changes according to

human activity and behaviour, and present clothes that encourage a different perspective on existing values, environments, and information. Recent projects include 'Photography and Fashion Since the 1990s,' Tokyo Photographic Art Museum (Tokyo, 2020); 'Never Lonely,' Taka Ishii Gallery (Tokyo, 2020); and 'MOT Annual 2019 Echo after Echo: Summoned Voices, New Shadows,' Museum of Contemporary Art Tokyo (Tokyo, 2019).

Eloise Rapp (b. 1984) is a designer and sustainability specialist. She currently works as a sustainability manager for a suite of Australian fashion labels and directs her responsible textile studio, Push Pull Textiles. Previously she taught at University of Technology Sydney, UNSW, Sydney, and Tainan National University of the Arts, Taiwan. Working at the intersection of textile craft and system change, her projects build a vision of viable alternatives to extractive production methods. Recent exhibitions include 'Mass Reduction,' Australian Tapestry Workshop (Melbourne, 2022) and 'Gingham All You've Got,' Australian Design Centre (Sydney, 2021).

Rapp lives and works on unceded Wangal Land in Sydney, Australia.
www.pushpulltextiles.com

Liam Revell (b. 1974) is an independent fashion designer, researcher, and educator. Revell's design practice contemplates decoration as an organizing principle having the capacity to affect the design, production, and appearance of garments and influence the construction of fashionable identity. His PhD, 'Fragments of an Aesthetic' (2021), was an experimental, process-focussed investigation of ideation exploiting the poetic qualities of words to inform an exploration of aesthetics. Exhibitions include 'The First Cut,' Project Space (Melbourne, 2011) and 'The Sea Between Us,' Tasma Terrace (Melbourne, 2018).

Revell lives and works in Melbourne, Australia.

Harriette Richards is a lecturer in Fashion Enterprise at RMIT University, Melbourne. She is co-founder of the Critical Fashion Studies research group and co-host of the Critical Fashion Studies podcast. Her work has most recently been

published in *Cultural Studies, Australian Feminist Studies* and *Gender, Work and Organization*. In 2021, she co-edited with Natalya Lusty and Rimi Khan, the 'Fashion Futures' special issue of *Continuum: Journal of Media and Cultural Studies*.

Richards is a Pākehā New Zealander who lives and works in Melbourne (AU).
www.harrietterichards.com

Nicole K. Rivas (b. 1990) is a fashion historian with an MA in Fashion Studies from Parsons The New School for Design; a BA in Studio Art/Art History from UC Riverside, California; and a MSLIS (Master of Science in Library and Information Science) Archival Studies scholar at St John's University, Queens NY. Rivas' interest is to preserve stories in cultural heritage using fashion objects for research needs in this never-ending forward movement of time.

Recent projects include: 'A Virtual Conversation with Fashion Archivists,' The Archivists Round Table of Metropolitan New York, Inc. (New York, 2022); 'Secondhand Cultures in Unsettled Times,' Cardiff University (2021). Past exhibitions include: 'Un:Resolved,' Parsons The New School for Design (New York, 2021); 'The School of Fashion,' Milk Gallery (New York, 2014); 'Designing The Second Skin: Giorgio di Sant'Angelo 1971–1991,' Sheila C. Johnson Design Center (New York, 2012).

Rivas lives in New York and works as an independent researcher, freelance archivist, collections specialist, and educator for various institutions.
www.nkrivas.com

Todd Robinson (b. 1971) is an interdisciplinary researcher, designer, artist, and senior lecturer in Fashion and Textiles at University of Technology Sydney. He researches the relationship between fashion and the body and advances embodied perspectives in the field of Fashion Studies. His research derives from long-term engagement with issues of fashion and the body, informed by work as a designer in the 1990s and early 2000s. His research is published in *Fashion Theory, International Journal of Fashion Studies, and Fashion Practice.*
www.somapoiesis.net.au

Mikhail Rojkov (b. 1996) is a researcher and a sustainable fashion advocate who graduated from HEAD–Genève. His areas of interest includes degrowth theory, (craft-) hacktivism, and investigative journalism. Recent publications include 'Radical acts of love,' *ISSUE* (2022); 'Wanna be a fashion doctor, my friend?,' TikTok (2022); 'Replace clothes with love,' HEAD (2021).

Rojkov lives and works in Geneva, Switzerland. He is currently developing a proposal for his city on a circular economy processing facility for end-of-life textiles.

Martine Rose established her label in 2007. She is inspired by her Jamaican-British heritage and her deep interest and personal involvement in the music cultures of London. The brand is sold in luxury boutiques worldwide and has been featured in art and fashion publications such as *032c, Arena Homme Plus, Vogue, Dazed and Confused, Fantastic Man, Kaleidoscope, i-D, POP* and *T magazine* among others.

In 2019, Martine Rose participated in the exhibition 'Get Up, Stand Up Now'—a major celebration of fifty years of Black British creativity at Somerset House in London. That year she was also nominated for the BFC's Menswear Designer of Year and the Urban Lux Award. Martine Rose was nominated for the BFC's British Menswear Designer of the Year award in 2018 and 2017, when she was also shortlisted for the LVMH prize and nominated for the ANDAM award for emerging designers.
www.martine-rose.com

Shanzhai Lyric is a body of research focusing on radical logistics and linguistics through the prism of technological aberration and nonofficial cultures. The project takes inspiration from the experimental English of shanzhai t-shirts made in China (proliferating across the globe) to examine how the language of counterfeit uses mimicry, hybridity, and permutation to both revel in and reveal the artifice of global hierarchies. Through an ever-growing archive of poetry-garments, Shanzhai Lyric explores the potential of mis-translation and nonsense as utopian world-making (breaking), previously in the form of poetry-lecture, essay, and installation.
www.shanzhailyric.info

Soft Baroque's Nicholas Gardner (b. 1988) and **Saša Štucin** (b. 1984) work simultaneously in object design and art. Their practice focuses on creating work with conflicting functions and imagery, without abandoning beauty or consumer logic. They are keen to blur the boundaries between acceptable furniture typologies and conceptual representative objects.

Recent exhibitions include: 'We Walked the Earth' with Uffe Isolotto, 59th Venice Biennale—Danish Pavilion (Venice, 2022); 'Total Space,' Museum für Gestaltung (Zürich, 2020); 'Sun City,' Milan, 2021; 'World of Ulteriors,' Etage Projects (Copenhagen, 2019). Recent contributions for publications include: 'Natural Order & Violent Hobbies' (2021); 'Tag Poems' (2020); 'Liquid Tension' (2020).

Gardner and Štucin live and work in Ljubljana.
www.softbaroque.com

Sihle Sogaula (b. 1993) is a material culture researcher who uses the curatorial to mediate relationships between the embodied, memory, and garments, both in archives and the quotidian. She is currently pursuing a MAFA at the Michaelis School of Fine Art, Cape Town, specializing in fashion curation and critique. Using found photographs, image-making, and garment-construction, Sogaula explores how material and immaterial objects become keepers of lived experiences, and how these records can be read, interpreted, and engaged. Recent publications include '(Re)collecting Lindro House of Fashion' (2021) and 'Ditaola' (co-edited with CCA Fellows of 2021).

Sihle Sogaula lives and works in Cape Town, South Africa.

Shanna Soh (b. 1978) is a design researcher, designer, and lecturer with a MA in Design Cultures from the VU Amsterdam. Currently, she teaches at the Royal Academy of Art, The Hague, NL (KABK) and Amsterdam Fashion Institute (AMFI). She considers her teaching environment as a (virtual) playground in which participants are encouraged to co-create experiments that question and reflect on the past, present, and future of design's ecosystems. Recent exhibitions include 'Making History: Pluriverse

Perspectives on Fashion & Textile Design Studies,' Research Catalogue, 2022.

Soh lives and works in Amsterdam and The Hague (NL).
www.schonevormen.nl

Vidmina Stasiulytė (b. 1984) is a researcher, senior lecturer, and artist whose work merges the field of radical aesthetics, sonic expression, and social inclusion. She holds a PhD from The Swedish School of Textiles, where she continues working as a senior lecturer and leads the research project 'Sonic Fashion' granted by The Swedish Research Council. Stasiulytė's research takes a radical approach to fashion by drawing on the non-visual, temporal expression-sound. It critiques the defining and designing practices by suggesting ways to include marginalized and differently-abled bodies towards a more inclusive and democratic fashion.

Recent exhibitions include: 'DRAFTS: Communicating Knowledge through Design Research Artifacts,' designtransfer (Berlin, 2022); 'UFNA: 1st International Art Triennial Unpredictable Futures,' Lithuanian Museum of Ethnocosmology (Molėtai, 2021); 'DRAFTS: Design Research Artifacts as an Intermediary Knowledge,' Pakistan Institute of Fashion and Design (Lahore, 2021); 'Sound to Wear,' Textile Museum (Borås, SE, 2021).

Recent publications include: 'Listening to Clothing: from Sonic Fashion Archive to Sonic Fashion Library,' *The Senses and Society* (2022): 1–11; 'Introducing Sensory-material Aesthetics in Textile Design Education,' *Diseña*, 20 (2022): 7–7, co-edited with Erin Lewis; 'UFNA: 1st International Art Triennial Unpredictable Futures.' *DRAFTS: Design Research Artifacts in the Context of Exhibition* (2022), co-edited with Faseeh Saleem, Egle Ganda Bogdanienė, Solveiga Gutautė, and Saulė Mažeikaitė-Teiberė; 'Sound-Based Thinking and Design Practices with Embodied Extensions,' *Proceedings of the Fourteenth International Conference on Tangible, Embedded, and Embodied Interaction* (2020): 889–892, co-edited with Erin Lewis;

Stasiulytė lives and works in Sweden.
www.vidmina.net, www.sonic-fashion.se

Johanna Tagada Hoffbeck (b. 1990) is a painter, transdisciplinary artist, and cultural practitioner. Her practice includes painting, drawing, installation, sculpture, film, photography, and writing; it often conceals ecological messages, rendered in soft and delicate methods. In Tagada's projects interaction with the environment and others plays a central role.

Recent solo exhibitions include: 'Dreaming About Tomorrow,' Nidi Gallery (Tokyo, 2022) and 'Meeting,' Pon Ding (Taipei, 2020). Recent publications include *Daily Practice* (2018), *Do Insects Play?* (2019) and *Work The Soul Must Have* (2022).

Tagada lives and works in rural Oxfordshire (England). www.johannatagada.net

Sang Thai (b. 1979) is a designer, lecturer, and creative practice researcher at RMIT University based in the lands of the Wurundjeri people. He holds degrees in both Architecture (from the University of Melbourne) and Fashion Design (from RMIT University) and has extensive industry design experience. Thai is currently a PhD candidate in the School of Fashion and Textiles at RMIT University with an interest in masculinity, intersectionality, and inclusive fashion design practices for social change. Recent publications include: '"All Tee, No Shade": A manifesto for a subtle critical practice negotiating queer, East Asian masculinities through T-shirts,' *Critical Studies in Men's Fashion* (2021); 'Designing for Drag,' in *Fashion Education: The Systemic Revolution* (Intellect Books, 2023). www.yellowishfever.com

Anne Karine Thorbjørnsen (b. 1982) is an artist and fashion designer. She works sculpturally with textiles and concrete through drapery, looking at the fold. She graduated with her BA and MA from Central Saint Martins, London (2012), where she set up her own practice before moving to Norway in 2015. Upcoming and previous exhibitions include: 'objets de la mode,' Oppland Kunstsenter (Lillehammer, NO, 2022); 'Oslo City #8 Fashion Edition,' BO (Oslo, 2022); 'studies of drapery,' Salgshallen (Oslo, 2021); 'Works in progress. No title,' Salgshallen (Oslo, 2020); 'SS18 Femmi,' The Community (Paris, 2017); 'AW16 Ffolds,' Diorama (Oslo, 2016); 'AW16 Ffolds,'

Amaze (Stockholm, 2016); 'Arcades,' Centre for Style at Bus Projects (Melbourne, 2013). Her work is part of the collection at The National Museum of Art Oslo, Buskerud Kunstsenter Drammen (NO) as well as private collections. Her fashion collections were stocked at stores such as Rare Market (Seoul) and IT (Hong Kong).

Thorbjørnsen lives and works in Elverum (NO). www.annekarinethorbjornsen. com

Clemens Thornquist is professor in Fashion Design at the Swedish School of Textiles, University of Borås (SE). His research spans fashion, art, and philosophy and aims to develop design foundations through experimental research. The main focus of this research is on the methodological developments and explorations of foundational definitions at the intersection between body, dress, and space.

Amy Twigger Holroyd (b. 1979) is a designer, maker, researcher, writer, and associate professor of Fashion and Sustainability at Nottingham School of Art & Design. Her current project, 'Fashion Fictions,' brings people together to create, experience, and reflect on engaging fictional visions of alternative fashion cultures to generate new perspectives on real-world systems. Recent publications include *Historical Perspectives on Sustainable Fashion: Inspiration for Change*, with Jennifer Farley Gordon and Colleen Hill (Bloomsbury Publishing, 2023).

Twigger Holroyd lives and works in Nottingham, UK. www.amytwiggerholroyd.com

Jeppe Ugelvig (b. 1993) is a theorist and curator. He completed his MA in Curatorial Studies at the Center for Curatorial Studies, Bard College, NY, and is a current PhD candidate at UC Santa Cruz, California. His research focuses on artistic practices within consumer capitalism, which was the topic of his first book, *Fashion Work 1993–2019* (Damiani, 2020). Recent exhibitions include 'The Endless Garment' at X Museum (Beijing, China). He is the founding editor of *Viscose*, a journal for fashion criticism and research. jeppeugelvig.com

Alessandra Vaccari is associate professor at Iuav University of Venice. Her research and teaching interests are in the area of fashion history and theory. With a background in contemporary art history, she works at the interface between visual studies and design history. Her publications include: *Time in Fashion* (co-edited with Caroline Evans) (Bloomsbury Visual Arts, 2020), *La moda nei discorsi dei designer* [Fashion in designers' discourse] (Clueb, 2012); *Fashion at the Time of Fascism* (co-edited with Mario Lupano) (Damiani, 2009).

Vaccari lives and works in Venice. www.iuav.it/Ateneo1/docenti/ design-e-a/docenti-st/Vaccari-Al/index.htm

Aurélie Van de Peer (b. 1986) (PhD) is a philosopher and sociologist with a special interest in how temporality is employed as a political tool in fashion as a concept, industry, and cultural phenomenon. Her work has appeared in academic outlets such as *Cultural Sociology*, *Fashion Theory*, *International Journal of Cultural Studies* and the edited books *Time in Fashion* (Bloomsbury, 2020) and *Insights on Fashion Journalism* (Taylor & Francis, 2022). She teaches as part of the MA Critical Fashion Practices at ArtEZ University of the Arts, Arnhem (NL).

Aurélie lives and works in Ghent (Belgium). www.aurelievandepeer.be

Adele Varcoe is an artist who lectures in the School of Fashion and Textiles at RMIT University, Melbourne. She creates transformative experiences that explore the social and emotional effects of fashion. A list of selected exhibitions include: 'Onesie World,' MONA, (Tasmania, 2018 and 2019); 'Wowzzzeee,' Arts House (Melbourne, 2018); Fremantle Festival (Fremantle, AU, 2019); 'Feelings of Undress, The Future of Fashion is Now,' Boijmans Van Beuningen Museum (Rotterdam, 2014).

Varcoe lives and works in Melbourne. www.adelevarcoe.com

Femke de Vries works as an artist and researcher. She lectures at ArtEZ MA Critical Fashion Practices, Arnhem (NL), and is a co-founder of Warehouse, a place for clothes in context in Amsterdam. Her practice mainly

revolves around addressing the dominant industrial and commercial workings of fashion and the exploration of alternatives. Recent publications include: *Dictionary Dressings* (Onomatopee, 2016); *What to buy for the fashion—focused reader in your life* (Warehouse, 2020, reprint 2021) and *A Magazine Reader* (co-edited with Hanka van der Voet) (Onomatopee, 2018–2022).
www.femkedevries.com

Ferdinand Waas (b. 1998) is an artist and researcher. He studied architecture (TU Vienna), social-cultural anthropology (Universität Wien, AT) and is currently studying Fine Arts (Royal Academy of Art, The Hague, NL). Waas works with a method of participatory observation to form(ulate) within the vocabulary of a given place or medium, a focus on retracing and storytelling of invisible systems and structures through elements of the daily and the ordinary.

Recent shows include: 'But s/he indorsed the sheen,' Vrij Palais (Amsterdam, 2022); 'Tread Carefully,' Einar Jonsson Museum (Reykjavik, IS, 2022); 'opening hours,' Treptower Ateliers (Berlin, 2022); 'take over,' Kunsthal Extra City (Antwerp, BE, 2022); 'James P. Sullivan, the soul of the tragedy is the prolonging of the uncertainty as much as possible,' h__s (Antwerp, BE, 2022); 'UA006050455LV' white box KHIO (Oslo, 2021).

Waas lives and works in The Hague (NL).

Beata Wilczek (b. 1986) is a researcher, educator, and strategist specializing in building projects for digital, diverse, and sustainable fashion futures. She is a founder and director at Unfolding Strategies and head of Impact at The Dematerialised. Wilczek is pursuing a PhD in Fashion Studies at ADBK Wien (Academy of Fine Arts, Vienna) and hosts the Fashion Knowledge podcast. She has been teaching for over ten years at various universities worldwide and has held a guest professorship at the University of Virginia (US).
www.beatawilczek.net

Lillian Wilkie (b. 1987) is a writer, editor, publisher, and lecturer on fashion media at University of the Arts, London. She is director of Chateau International, an imprint producing books, zines, and editions in collaboration with artists, writers, educators, and project spaces. She has written on photography and fashion and published for a range of titles including *Modern Matter, Elephant Magazine* and *C4 Journal*. Her book *The Origin of Springs* (2017) was published by Tenderbooks.

Wilkie lives and works in London.
www.chateauinternational.co.uk

Annie Wu is a designer, artist, and educator based in Melbourne. She has been working on and developing her fashion practice (and brand) Articles of Clothing for the last seven years—translating a numbering process that is often used in naming untitled or serial works of art into a sustainable fashion design process and archive. Currently there are 180 styles in this archive, and each style can be retrieved and re-produced at any time. Wu was trained in fine art and has studied and worked in the Netherlands and exhibited her work internationally. She is a lecturer in Fashion and Sustainability at the Australian College of the Arts.
www.articlesofclothing.com.au

Patricia Wu Wu is a fashion designer and researcher. She studied at the Glasgow School of Art and is currently nearing the completion of her PhD at Edinburgh College of Art. Her research explores how fashion can synthesize the geological timescales of the Anthropocene to the scale of the body. Working at the nexus of computational design, digital fabrication, and remote sensing, she has developed a data-driven form-making practice to make visible anthropogenic changes in Earth.

Recent exhibitions include: 'Futurescan 5,' University of Leeds (2022); 'Emerging Materialities,' Museu del Disseny (Barcelona, 2019). Recent publications include: 'AI and Emerging Digital Technologies as a Design Material,' *ELISAVA* (peer-reviewed journal) (2019); *Material Fluidity* (co-edited with Magdalena Lavin and Daniela Espinoza) (2019).
www.patriciawuwu.com

Every time a fashion magazine hits the newsstands, it contains hundreds of new images created specifically for that issue. Though this approach may not be unique to the fashion industry, fashion magazines have an elaborate tradition for creating custom-made imagery.

In the early process of designing *Radical Fashion Exercises* we were faced with the fact that most of the contributions did not include visuals to accompany the written exercises. Therefore the idea of creating custom-made imagery for this book came to mind, and I began to gather and produce (the majority of) the images you find in these pages. This visual layer combines snapshots and archival images, alongside some photos provided by the contributors.

The conceptual starting point for these images was inspired by 'how-to' manuals that give step-by-step visual directions on how to create something. The intention was to produce an image for each exercise that evokes an approach or atmosphere that supports the idea of the exercise—not one that demonstrates how to follow the instructions of the exercise. In this way, the visuals function as paratextual to the instructional texts.

Due to the disparate character of the images, the layout of *Radical Fashion Exercises* includes two characteristic graphic elements that are intended to visually bind the book together. Firstly, each chapter has its own visual seam—a graphic element that is attached to one side of each image and that simultaneously interrupts and connects the image to the page, like the sewn seam of a garment. Secondly, the headers are set in a dotted typeface that visually references the punch cards used to operate knitting and jacquard weaving machines.

—Line Arngaard

This book was the result of an international collaborative effort—an effort of the commons (as Astrid would say)— and we thank all who have been involved. To produce this book, over 360 submissions were collected via an Open Call. These submissions were then discussed at length, juried and edited. Our eternal gratitude is extended to the editorial team at Valiz, and especially Astrid Vorstermans and Pia Pol, who believed in the project and supported it from the beginning. We also thank the wonderful Line Arngaard for patiently following the book's progress and for making sense of its content with her thoughtful design and inventive approach to the book's images. We also thank our jury members for generously offering their time and insight, Anouk Beckers, heeten bhagat, Ruby Hoette, Ulrik Martin Larsen, and Jeppe Ugelvig. These panel members helped with the onerous and nuanced task of hewing the selection to the roughly one-hundred exercises found in the book.

We also wish to thank our colleagues and students at RMIT University, who we have worked alongside, learned from and with whom we have developed an understanding of how fashion can be radical.

Finally, we thank our partners, Cameron and Rowan, for their patience, support and criticality, manifested in the many discussions about the book along the way. Thank you also to baby Twyla, who was born while we put the book together, for quietly joining the editorial meetings. And, of course, we thank our cats, Citi, Tanuki and Mochi, for providing much-needed emotional support.

—Laura Gardner & Daphne Mohajer va Pesaran

Editors:
Laura Gardner &
Daphne Mohajer va Pesaran

Editorial advice:
Line Arngaard
Astrid Vorstermans

Copy-editing:
Liana Simmons

Index:
Laura Gardner &
Daphne Mohajer va Pesaran

Design and typesetting:
Line Arngaard

Typefaces:
Univers
Drunken Pixel

Paper inside:
Munken Print White, 90 gr 1.5

Paper cover:
Invercote, 200 gr

Lithography:
Mariska Bijl, Wilco Art Books,
Amersfoort

Printing and binding:
Wilco Art Books, Amersfoort

Publisher:
Valiz, Amsterdam, 2023
Astrid Vorstermans & Pia Pol,
www.valiz.nl

Creative Commons BC-NC-ND 4.0
   The texts of this book are
licensed under a Creative
Commons Attribution-NonCom-
mercial- NoDerivativesWorks
4.0 international licence.
   You are free to: Share, copy
and redistribute the material
in any medium or format. The
licensor cannot revoke these
freedoms as long as you follow
the license terms. Under the
following terms:
   — Attribution
   — NonCommercial
   — NoDerivatives
   — No additional restrictions
   The full license can be found
at creativecommons.org/licens-
es/by-nc-nd/4.0

International distribution
NL/LU: Centraal Boekhuis,
www.centraal.boekhuis.nl

BE: EPO, www.epo.be

GB/IE: Central Books,
www.centralbooks.com

Europe (excl. GB/IE/BE/NL)/Asia:
Idea Books, www.ideabooks.nl

USA/Canada/Latin America:
D.A.P., www.artbook.com

Australia: Perimeter Books,
www.perimeterbooks.com

Individual orders: www.valiz.nl;
info@valiz.nl

This publication has been printed on FSC-certified paper by an
FSC-certified printer. The FSC,
Forest Stewardship Council
promotes environmentally
appropriate, socially beneficial,
and economically viable man-
agement of the world's forests.
www.fsc.org

Valiz is an independent international publisher, addressing
contemporary developments
in art, design, architecture,
and urban affairs. Their books
provide critical reflection and
interdisciplinary inspiration,
often establishing a connection
between cultural disciplines
and socio-economic questions.
www.valiz.nl
@valiz_books_projects

ISBN 978-94-93246-19-5
Printed and bound in the
Netherlands/EU, 2023